CONSISTENT CHRISTIANITY

We . . . pray for you, asking that you may . . . lead a life worthy of the Lord, fully pleasing to him, bearing fruit in every good work and increasing in the knowledge of God.

Colossians i.9,10, RSV.

Now the God of peace . . . make you perfect in every good work to do his will, working in you that which is wellpleasing in his sight, through Jesus Christ; to whom be glory for ever and ever. Amen.

Hebrews xiii.20,21.

CONSISTENT CHRISTIANITY

by

M. C. GRIFFITHS

LONDON
INTER-VARSITY FELLOWSHIP
39 BEDFORD SQUARE, W.C.1

PRINTED AND BOUND IN ENGLAND BY
HAZELL WATSON AND VINEY LTD
AYLESBURY AND SLOUGH

CONTENTS

ACKNOWLEDGEMENT

Scripture quotations from the Revised Standard Version of the Bible (copyright 1946 and 1952 by the Division of Christian Education, National Council of Churches, U.S.A.) are used by permission.

FOREWORD

THIS is not a book of answers. It is partly a book of problems and partly a blotted copybook; if it shows any insight into some inconsistent Christianity, then it is because the writer is conscious of failure at this point in his own life.

In the old fairy-tale the king's magic suit was visible only to those who knew it was supposed to be there. It is because our putting on of the 'new man' is sometimes scarcely discernible to the outside observer that this book was requested by Christian student leaders. Young converts may be orthodox in doctrine and eager to win others, may talk the same peculiar jargon and show some of the same behaviourisms as their elders; yet at the same time they often fail to show in a positive and attractive way the courtesy and winsomeness to be expected of a Christian. Their lives are too little different from those of the unbelievers around them.

I am acutely conscious of my own debt to those who both by practice and precept have shown me something of all that 'adorning the doctrine of God our Saviour' ought to mean. Many of the ideas that now seem part of my own thinking I owe, under God, to faithful teachers and friends. Especial thanks are due to Mr Nigel Sylvester for all his suggestions and criticisms, and to Mr Robert Ewan, Mr Leith Samuel and the Rev. Alan Stibbs for many stimulating ideas.

I trust that by the grace of God this book may be used to help me and those who read it to become truly consistent Christians who walk even as He walked.

M. C. G.

CHAPTER I

TOO HEAVENLY MINDED?

'WHAT are they for, Daddy?' is a question that we must often have asked as children. One wonders what our answer would be if we were asked: 'What are Christians for?' Far too many of us are smugly content with the fact that we are Christians, without ever considering the purpose of our existence. Judging by our customary attitude, our reply to the question would be, 'Christians are made to go to heaven, of course!', for our tendency is to place far more emphasis upon *where* the *next* life is to be spent than upon *how* this *present* life is to be spent. But our imaginary child questioner, with some impatience at grown-up obtuseness, would inevitably ask the supplementary question: 'Yes, but *now*, I mean. Here on earth.'

In all probability, however—such is our adult preoccupation with the 'where-will-you-spend-eternity?' problem—we may never have thought about the question at all. We have faithfully proclaimed that today is the day of salvation, but have frequently forgotten to tell the young convert what tomorrow is for. Or, again, we have emphasized the sphere of glory prepared for us to occupy hereafter, rather than the sphere of good works prepared for us to occupy here and now. The Bible teaches that God has prepared a place for the Christian in both spheres (see e.g., 1 Pet. i.4; Eph. ii.10). It is simply because so much evangelical thinking seems to regard this earth as a mere waiting-room for heaven, that it is necessary to stress the fact that our life here on earth *is* important. It is not just an unfortunate interval during which we are to twiddle our thumbs until we are 'called up higher'. The Christian is not intended to be a sort of sanctified 'white elephant'.

THIS WORLD

Part of the trouble is due to a one-sided doctrine of 'this world'. Christians have noted those passages which treat of the world as being in darkness, waiting for the dawning of the day (Rom. xiii.12), and have come to think of life as a weary pilgrimage through what is called this 'wilderness scene'. The Victorian hymn-writer's conception :

> Earth is a desert drear,
> Heaven is my home,

originating in a comparison between the Israelite wanderings after the Exodus and our experience after conversion, has become part of our evangelical jargon. It is as well to recognize, however, that some scriptural statements are relative. This is best illustrated from a more obvious example in Luke xiv.26 where we read : 'If any man come to me, and hate not his father, and mother, and wife, and children . . . he cannot be my disciple.' Here the Christian is told to hate his wife ; but elsewhere the Christian husband is told to love his wife as Christ also loved the Church and gave Himself for it (Eph. v.25). Clearly, then, the Christian is to love his wife very dearly indeed ; but even such love as this will be as hatred compared with his love for the Lord. Our love for the Lord is to be such that, *in comparison*, the finest human love, for wife or family, may be described as 'hatred'. Similarly it may be argued that this world is a gloomy wilderness only *in comparison* with the glory which shall be revealed.

One hears some Christians speak so slightingly of 'this world' that they are, in fact, guilty of disparaging what God in His providence has created. For 'God saw everything that he had made, and, behold, it was very good'. In spite of the fall, and the resultant 'groaning' and 'travailing' of the whole creation (Rom. viii. 18–23), this quality of 'very goodness' has not entirely disappeared. See how the psalmist is able to rejoice in God's creation and His material provision for His creatures (Ps. civ), or note the oft-repeated refrain 'The earth is the Lord's, and the fulness thereof' (Pss. xxiv. 1, l. 12, etc.). Isaiah's great vision of the Lord, high and lifted up, was accompanied by the cry : 'Holy, holy, holy, is the Lord of hosts : the whole *earth* is full of his glory.' It is worth noting that the passages which have the other emphasis, reminding us that here we have no 'continuing city', or pointing out the transient nature of this world, are usually written in the context of Christians suffering hardship or persecution, and who need, therefore, to be encouraged with the reminder that God has much better things in store. These truths must be held in proper balance. We must certainly never stress what is to come in such a way as to suggest that what we do here and now does not matter. It was our Lord Himself who instructed us to pray, 'Thy will be done *in earth*, as it is in heaven'. What we do here on this earth and in this world is very important.

To put our question in another way : Why are

Christians left on earth at all? Why are they not whisked off to heaven as soon as they are converted? In so much Christian teaching there is a great hiatus between conversion and entry into the next world. How are we to occupy this interval? What is this life for?

PRACTICAL HOLINESS

'God hath ... called us ... unto holiness' (1 Thes. iv.7). He leaves us on earth in order that we may grow in holiness, or, as the 1928 Prayer Book has it, in order that we may have 'time for amendment of life'. Christians are not to relax complacently in their arm-chairs and merely rejoice in being saved. We are meant to be 'perfecting holiness in the fear of God' (2 Cor. vii.1). That is one of the things we are here for. When we first come in faith, trusting in the Saviour for forgiveness, we are given the right to go to heaven. From then on, throughout the remainder of our earthly lives, God works in us so that, little by little, we may be made more *fit* to go to heaven. He first reckons us righteous through justification, in order that He may actually make us righteous by sanctification. In the former act, Christ's righteous-ness is imputed to us at a certain moment of time, while in the latter process His righteousness is actu-ally imparted to us over a period of time. God first credits His righteousness, as it were, to our account, and then He actually brings us into an enjoyment of what He has given. Sanctification is thus an intended consequence of justification. If a man says that he has been converted, then we shall expect to find him becoming more and more sanctified as the days go by. This is a major theme of Scripture, as a few selected examples will show.

Where the Old Testament expresses God's intention that His people should live holy lives, we find that obedience to the Commandments is not asked in isolation, but as a consequence of the redemption which God has already effected for His people. 'I am the Lord thy God, which have brought thee out of the land of Egypt, out of the house of bondage', and, therefore, 'Thou shalt have no other gods before me', and so on. The Lord's moral laws for His people spring from the fact that He has redeemed them and made them His own. Because He is holy, then those who belong to Him must be holy too. The whole theme of the Old Testament, of the law and prophets, is that the holy Lord expects His people to be holy. The prophets are sent to rebuke the people for failing to live as the people of God should live. We cannot evade this argument by saying that they lived before the days when God's grace was made plain by the redemption through the Lord Jesus. The Old Testament is full of expressions of the grace of God, which was to be shown forth in the death of the Lord Jesus, the efficacy of which was retrospective as well as prospective (Rom. iii.25).

In any case, we cannot make a distinction between the old and new covenants in this way, since the New Testament likewise expects holiness from those who are redeemed and forgiven sinners. Our Lord teaches that the righteousness of the citizens of the kingdom is to exceed that of the scribes and Pharisees (Mt. v.20). The tree is expected to bring forth good fruit if it is not to be hewn down (Mt. vii.19). The branch of the vine that brings forth no fruit will be cast forth and burned (Jn. xv.6). The emphasis here is on the fruitful life of righteousness. The 'blessed of my Father' who inherit the kingdom are those who feed the hungry, give drink to the thirsty, take in strangers, clothe the naked and who visit the sick and the prisoners (Mt. xxv.34–40). This holiness is extremely practical in its expression. It is very 'down to earth'; and it is what the Lord Jesus looks for as the evidence of a real faith. The New Testament seems to have no place for the man who claims to be a believer, but who is wilfully and persistently inconsistent (Jas. ii.14–17; 1 Jn. ii.3–6).

This same note is struck in the apostolic teaching given to the Church in the Epistles. Because God's character is holy, then we must be holy too (1 Pet. i.15). Because God has acted in redemption, then a new life must spring out of it (1 Cor. vi.20). Because the Christian's body is the temple of the Holy Spirit, it must not be defiled (1 Cor. iii.16, 17). Because the Lord is returning for His people, what manner of persons ought we to be? (2 Pet. iii.11–14.) Note that we never find what might be called 'theoretical' doctrine placed in isolation in the New Testament. Every great Bible doctrine has its inevitable corollary in practical conduct. The latter part of each of the Epistles is almost entirely taken up with directions for righteous Christian living. Our eyes have come so close to the leaves of our Bibles that we can scarcely see the trees, let alone the wood! We have been scrutinizing every word in an effort to delve deeper into the doctrines of Scripture, when what we sometimes need to do is to step back and view the larger canvas of the whole sweep of God's purposes for men on earth.

EVANGELISM

In answering the question 'Why are Christians left on earth?', most of us would leap to the reply that it was because of the necessity of witness and the task of world evangelization. The gospel is to be proclaimed through human agency. We are to obey our Lord's parting command to 'go therefore and make disciples of all nations'. But we are in danger of getting even this great truth out of perspective. Even if there were no-one to be evangelized, we should still have to live holy lives. Peter, in his first Epistle, using imagery taken from the Old Testament, suggests that Christians are, first and foremost, to be a 'holy priesthood, to offer up spiritual sacrifices, acceptable to God by Jesus Christ'. This is not uncommonly expounded purely in terms of formal worship. But surely this passage means that the whole life of the Christian is to be a 'living sacrifice'. Thus the writer to the Hebrews says, 'By him therefore let us offer the sacrifice of praise to God continually, that is, the fruit of our lips giving thanks to his name' (xiii.15).

Secondly, Peter declares that Christians are to be a 'holy nation, God's own people, that you may declare the wonderful deeds of him who called you out of darkness into his marvellous light' (1 Pet. ii.9, RSV). This idea likewise is commonly limited to 'telling others', so that taking these two verses together the great Christian duties are seen as worship and witness. But the emphasis here is not primarily upon winning others, but rather that 'the heathen shall know that I am the Lord . . . when I shall be sanctified in you before their eyes'; i.e. it is the whole manner of life of God's people which is to be the evidence of their belonging to Him. Similarly Peter implies that *the whole life* of the Christian is involved, not simply evangelism in the restricted sense of speaking to others. The whole life of the Christian is to be worship and the whole life of the Christian is to be witness : they are not merely things which he does, or in which he participates.

Sanctification is an essential implementation of evangelism. The transformed life of the Christian should be one of the most convincing evidences of divine intervention in human affairs. T. R. Glover wrote : 'The early Christian Church succeeded so magnificently because they outlived, out-thought and outdied the pagan world.' Today we, too, must beat the pagan world at living and show them that only when they become Christians can they live as men were meant to live. A recent broadcast finished with the words : 'Industrial man is not a god. Indeed, his trouble is that he is not even a man. It is our task to find man again. Anything less than that will not be enough.' No real solution was offered by the speaker, but as Christians we know that only God the Creator can make us into real men. It is by our lives alone that we can show that this is no empty boast.

Such evidence of changed lives may convince where all the preaching of eternal realities may fail. When you are judging Christianity by the difference it will make in life at the present moment, promises of 'pie in the sky when you die' are not really acceptable. Evidence here and now, rather than there and then, is what men are looking for. We must be living demonstrations that eternal life is not some future benefit to be received at death or enjoyed after death, but a present experience to be received at conversion and enjoyed thereafter.[1] The Christian is to enjoy these benefits now as well as later on. He can eat his cake *and* have it! Daily practical sanctification of life has as big a part to play in evangelism, then, as has direct proclamation of the gospel.

A DISTORTED EMPHASIS

There has been a tendency in some of our churches to distort this scriptural balance. This has resulted in an emphasis upon evangelism without a proper complement of practical teaching on the Christian life. The doctrine of justification is apt to figure prominently in services for believers and unbelievers alike. Indeed, it is accorded a prominence disproportionate to that which it enjoys in Scripture. Young converts have been known to complain of a certain sameness in the sermons they hear : 'Ten thousand thousand are their texts, but all their sermons one.' Of course we rejoice in the old, old story, but are we really being given a full balance of Scripture teaching in our churches? One hears very little in the way of an evangelical doctrine of the Christian life today. There is very little which is equivalent to the second half of the Epistles. Paul was able to say to the Ephesian elders, concerning his ministry in their city: 'I kept back nothing that was profitable unto you . . . I have not shunned to declare unto you all the counsel of God. . . .' Are we keeping back part of the

[1] See Jn. v.24: '. . . *hath* everlasting life . . . *is* passed from death unto life.' Jn. x.10: '. . . I am come that they might have life, and that they might have it more abundantly.' 1 Jn. v.12: 'He that hath the Son *hath* life.'

Word of God that we pride ourselves so much on preaching?

We sometimes hear strange sanctification doctrines concocted from verses torn willy-nilly from their contexts, which seem to be aimed at making the practical instructions of Scripture redundant. It is suggested that holiness is to be achieved by an 'experience', rather than by practical obedience to the will of God. If this were the case, one wonders why Paul never said so, and why he wasted so much papyrus in giving us practical and mundane instruction for the details of everyday life. This book is an attempt to remind ourselves of the practical aspect of Christian holiness. There is the danger of engendering, among young people today, a type of Christianity in which more attention is paid to evangelism and to doctrine than to the standard of living which the Bible enjoins. There is more emphasis, too, on what may be called the negative aspects of holiness—on separation from the world—and not enough on positive holy living within the world.

REASONS FOR THIS NEGLECT

Why have Protestant Christians neglected the doctrine of the Christian life and left the field so much to writers known as 'Catholic'? It has not always been so. Like other Puritan writers, Richard Baxter supplies in his *Christian Directory* a wealth of practical teaching, with detailed directions for all sorts of situations; for example, he gives counsel as to what a wife should do if her husband loses his temper, and vice versa. Primarily the neglect of the doctrine of holy living seems to have been a reaction against those who, having no saving gospel of grace and redemption through the blood of Christ, preach a gospel of works, a social gospel, or who offer 'pitiful little homilies' [1] of a moral character instead. We have very rightly reacted against those who conceive of 'Mission' in terms of 'cultural reintegration over a long period' and 'the conversion of the community as a whole'. But, while deprecating those who have no saving gospel for the individual, we must not forget that the true biblical gospel does have social and ethical consequences.

Secondly, this failure to be fully scriptural often arises from a fear of being thought not to have preached the gospel! In my own student days it was fashionable to criticize any sermon which did not enlarge upon sin, the cross and how to become a Christian, as though every sermon must contain these ingredients irrespective of what passage of Scripture was being expounded. We were fast becoming advocates of impository, rather than expository, preaching. Surely in our reaction against those who never preach for conversion, it is foolish to go to the opposite extreme and never preach about anything else! Perhaps it is this distorted view of the content of the Christian gospel which explains the not uncommon excuse of non-Christians that they fail to see any difference between the lives of Christians and their own. If Christians have evangelistic services for breakfast, dinner, lunch and tea—then no wonder there is a dietary deficiency in the matter of day-to-day living. It is of little use telling the unbeliever what a difference it makes to be a Christian if he cannot see something of it for himself.

[1] A descriptive phrase coined by the Bishop of Rochester.

THE PLACE OF GOOD WORKS

It is assumed that the reader is perfectly clear that we cannot earn forgiveness by good works or be justified by any merits of our own, but only through trusting in the Lord Jesus, who shed His blood for us. 'By grace are ye saved through faith; and that not of yourselves : it is the gift of God : not of works, lest any man should boast. For we are his workmanship, created in Christ Jesus unto good works, which God hath before ordained that we should walk in them' (Eph. ii.8–10). The place of works is here very clearly defined ; not 'of works' as meriting or earning justification, but 'unto good works' as the evidence and the natural outcome of justification. We have not become God's children by holy living, but, because He has now made us His children by adoption, such a holy life is expected of us. He 'will be a Father unto you, and ye shall be my sons and daughters, saith the Lord Almighty. Having therefore these promises, dearly beloved, let us cleanse ourselves from all filthiness of the flesh and spirit, perfecting holiness in the fear of God' (2 Cor. vi.18–vii.1).

James, in a famous passage, urges that a true faith is evidenced by works. Mere profession of faith—simply 'to say' that one has faith—is not enough. There must be accompanying works. 'As the body without the spirit is dead, so faith without works is dead also' (Jas. ii.14–26). Much is sometimes made of an alleged difference between James and Paul here ; but Paul says the same thing in the Epistle to Titus. He emphasizes that salvation is 'not by works of righteousness which we have done' (Tit. iii.5), but at the same time denounces those who 'profess that they know God; but in works they deny him' (Tit. i.16). Paul goes on to say that our Saviour's purpose in giving Himself to redeem us from all iniquity was to 'purify unto himself a people for his own possession, zealous of good works' (Tit. ii.14, RV), and urges Titus to 'affirm constantly, that they which have believed in God might be careful to maintain good works' (Tit. iii.8).

This book is an attempt to follow Titus in affirming constantly that we Christians need to pay close attention to our manner of life here on earth. God has a purpose for us. We are to be perfecting holiness. In the chapters which follow we shall consider what this quest for holiness means in practical, everyday terms.

CHAPTER II

SPLIT PERSONALITY?

A NOTICE saying 'Divine service is conducted here four times daily' was seen, not on the notice-board of a 'super-keen' church, but hanging over a scullery sink! The lady who put it there obviously had the right attitude to washing-up, an attitude which should be extended to the whole of the Christian life.

The wrong attitude is common among Christians who often speak as though the activities of this present life were to be divided into things 'spiritual' and things 'secular'. Thus, part of our life is spent 'spiritually'—at innumerable meetings, in personal prayer and Bible reading, in public worship and in 'profitable' conversation with men about their souls. The rest of our time, however, must, perforce, be spent in a less worthy way on 'the things of this world'—eating, drinking, sleeping, working, play-ing, being with our families, digging in the garden, having holidays and so forth. Such a view overlooks the fact that God in His providence has so ordered our lives that they must normally include all these commonplace activities. Surely, then, He has some purpose in so doing.

The teaching of Scripture is simple : 'So, whether you eat or drink, or whatever you do, do all to the glory of God' (1 Cor. x.31, RSV). Can even such mundane operations as are essential to the main-tenance of our bodies be done to God's glory? The principle of Scripture is that everything we do is to be done to this end, and if there are things we cannot do to His glory, then they are things that we ought not to be doing at all. Our life is not to be divided into two watertight compartments. Everything we do must be regarded as part of the Christian life. To grasp this thrilling truth transforms our lives, giving them a new integrity and harmony. To cling to the false dichotomy can spoil the simple joys of a happy home and hard work. Let me suggest some of the effects of this 'heresy' upon our thinking.

A TENDENCY TO HYPOCRISY

The word translated 'hypocrite' in the New Testament means literally 'play-actor'; that is, those who play one part in the church and another in daily life. This division of our lives into two compartments leads straight to hypocrisy. We keep our religious life in one compartment and the rest of our life in the other. As a result, we see no need to relate what we hear in church on Sunday to the way we behave, or run our business, from Monday to Saturday. Our 'Sunday selves' are as neatly stored during the rest of the week as our 'Sunday suits' often are.

It is because of this kind of 'compartmentalization' that Hosea rebukes Ephraim for being 'a cake not turned' (Ho. vii.8). The art of cooking drop scones is to turn them over at the proper moment. If, being inattentive like King Alfred with his cakes, we fail to do this, one side will be overcooked while the other remains underdone. Israel had plenty of religion, plenty of sacrifices and burnt offerings; but the Lord values mercy towards men and knowledge of Himself more highly than those (Ho. vi.6). They failed to apply their religion to daily living and business. George Adam Smith writes on this: 'Of how many Christians is it true that they are but halfbaked —living a life one side of which reeks with the smoke of sacrifice, while the other is never warmed by one religious thought. We may have too much religion if we confine it to one day or one department of life: our worship overdone, with the sap and the freshness burnt out of it, cindery, dusty, unattractive, fit only for crumbling; our conduct cold, damp and heavy, like dough the fire has never reached.'[1]

Here again we see how such a false division of our lives results in inconsistency. The Christian himself may be ignorant of his hypocrisy, but unbelieving society is quick to notice the fault and to comment upon it. A man may be a noted speaker at conferences and convention meetings, and yet have a very different reputation in his home village. A young woman may sit regularly in the same seat in church, but have a different reputation in the factory or office. The respected elder or churchwarden may prove to be harsh and unscrupulous in his business methods. Nor is the difficulty of being utterly consistent confined only to these people, as we can all testify. The special difficulty for those of us who have only recently come to Christ is that there may be large areas of our lives which have not come under Christian cultivation, and are not yet bringing forth fruit to the glory of God. It is a known fact that some businesses keep two sets of books, one for themselves and one for the income-tax people. But none of us can keep a separate set of books for God; all things are naked and open to Him with whom we

[1] *Book of the Twelve Prophets,* Vol. I, p. 295.

have to do. He is not deceived by the play-actor who leads a double life.

A FALSE VIEW OF HOLINESS

If we adopt this division of life into sacred and secular, then it must follow that the more time we spend on 'spiritual things', the more holy we shall be. Is it not true that for some reason we tend to regard the vocation of the Christian minister or overseas missionary as being a cut above that of the ordinary run of believers? We instinctively feel, no doubt, that he can spend more time saying his prayers and reading his Bible. The common expression 'He's in full-time Christian work'[1] simply reeks of the idea that the work of some Christians is intrinsically more Christian than that of others, and that while some give all of their time to the service of God, others can give only part. But all Christians, whatever their employment, are full-time Christian workers. If we do not maintain this, we shall be in danger of having a caste system within the Church, a ruling hierarchy who lord it over their humbler brethren.

The first-century Jews appear to have held a similar idea, for they regarded the Pharisees as the whole-time holy men of the day. It is only the rich who can afford to be religious all the time, and if they are going to find it hard to get into the kingdom, what hope is there for the poor who have to labour at defiling tasks? 'Who then can be saved?' (See Lk. xviii.24–26.)

---

[1] A little experience of 'full-time Christian work' soon reveals how much time is spent in stoking fires, mending windows, 'changing' babies and other practical matters.

The medieval Church fell into a similar error in its attitude to monasticism (an error unfortunately revived in our own day). It was based upon the false premise that to spend the day in keeping the 'canonical hours', so that it became one long round of services (like many a Christian's Sunday!), was a more holy way of spending it than any other. If you adopt this premise it follows that the so-called 'religious' is therefore more holy than anyone else; and that if you want to be a really wholehearted Christian you must enter a monastery. Such teaching is quite unbiblical. It is very interesting that Brother Lawrence, himself a monk, should have remarked that he was more united with God during his ordinary activities than when he left them to engage in religious exercises, in which he was generally afflicted with spiritual dryness.[1] Growth in grace is not to be equated with the expansion of the religious compartment, but with the degree to which we are able to glorify God in all that we do. This should help to correct the Christian who thinks it more 'spiritual' to be in his bedroom reading his Bible than to be in the kitchen helping his mother with the washing-up, or to challenge him who considers it more 'profitable' to spend all of his vacation away at missions and camps than to stay at home with his family and get down to some academic work.

A WRONG ATTITUDE TO WORK

'Ordinary work' is often considered less honouring to God than 'Christian work'. The student may think he is right to engage in Christian Union activity,

[1] *The Practice of the Presence of God*, Third Conversation of Brother Lawrence (Attwater's translation).

attend multitudinous meetings, speak to others about Christ and all to the neglect of his academic work. But this attitude is wrong, and the student needs to realize that to be diligent in his academic studies *is* to engage in Christian work. The graduate may neglect his profession, his family or the constant reading needed to keep up to date, in the belief that it is more important to be spending long hours helping at local churches or Bible classes. We may be tempted to envy those who have a more interesting job than ours, coveting their responsibilities instead of faithfully fulfilling our own. Nevertheless, these attitudes also are contrary to what Scripture teaches. Those in monotonous or unskilled jobs may be tempted to regard their work as merely a way of earning their bread and butter. But the New Testament suggests rather, as someone has put it, that the tedium should be changed into a *Te Deum*.

It is noteworthy that much of the Bible's teaching about work is addressed to slaves. 'Whatever you do, put your whole heart and soul into it, as into work done for God, and not merely for men . . . you are actually employed by Christ, and not just by your earthly master' is Phillips' paraphrase of Colossians iii.23 f. If the humble drudgery of slaves admits of such consecration, how much more does any nobler form of human business. No lower duties can be imagined than those of a slave in a heathen family. Evasion rendered him liable to the brand, the lash and the treadmill. But though bound to this work by the most galling necessity, at the beck and call of a cruel master, the Christian slave is bidden to do it 'unto the Lord'. Whatever the Christian does is 'Christian work' and must be done for Christ. As

Protestants, we rejoice in expounding the great doctrine of the priesthood of all believers. We tend to concentrate, however, on its negative aspect; namely, that there is no place in any truly New Testament Christianity for a special caste of sacrificing priests, since the great atoning sacrifice of Christ has been made once and for all. But we must also go on to stress its positive application; namely, that every believer *is* a priest, who offers the sacrifice of praise continually in his daily life, in his work and in his home.

There is an interesting passage in Luther in which he says that God has called men to labour because He labours. He works at common occupations. God is a tailor, who makes a coat for the deer which lasts for a thousand years. He is a shoemaker, who provides boots the deer will not outlive. He is also a butler, who sets forth a feast for the sparrows and spends more on them annually than the total revenue of the King of France. And if God does these things, then surely we can honour Him in these humble callings also, and in many others beside. We may extend Luther's list, remembering Sir James Jeans' reference to God as a Mathematician. He is also the Master Physicist who thought out atomic physics, and the Master Biologist who thought out genetics. In our work we may work His work after Him, and in our studies we may think His thoughts after Him.

It is a wonderful and remarkable fact, that the commendation of the heavenly Voice—'This is my beloved Son, in whom I am well pleased'—is given before there is any record of miracles performed or sermons preached. He is commended as the Son of man for His perfect life, giving glory to God in the simple everyday life of a small provincial village, working as a local carpenter, living in a country home with his own humble family. We are told so little about those hidden years, but so much is suggested : 'Jesus increased in wisdom and stature, and in favour with God and man.' There are the little liftings of the curtain, which show Him taking part in the everyday joys and sorrows of the people; 'there was a marriage at Cana in Galilee, and the mother of Jesus was there; Jesus also was invited to the marriage, with his disciples' (RSV). It was in the simple life of home and workshop that the Lord Jesus pleased His heavenly Father in these early years, rather than in the exercise of His special messianic commission. What a challenge it is to readers under thirty years of age, who tend to think that later on, at some time in the future when they have attained to some prominence in Church or State, they will glorify their Lord, to realize that He expects them to glorify Him now in their own homes and places of work. We are told by the beloved disciple that we are to 'walk, even as he walked'. Would that our lives, as ordinary people in ordinary ways, might yet have something of that wonderful quality of the One who does all things well. The Father's work in creation, the Son's life among men and the Spirit's endowment of craftsmen with special gifts (Ex. xxxi.3, xxxv.31) all point to this high view of the consecration of labour.

Thus Paul labours at his tentmaking, Lydia in the making of purple and Simon at his tanning, and there is nothing to suggest that Zacchaeus was bidden to leave his tax-collecting, Cornelius his military service or Sergius Paulus the service of the Roman government. Every man is exhorted in the calling wherein he is called, therein to 'abide with God' (1 Cor. vii.24; cf. 2 Thes. iii.10; Eph. iv.28). We are to abide in our profession *with* God, our hand in His, whether we are called as tinker or tailor, soldier or sailor (though not, of course, as beggarman or thief!). This is the normal position, although He may call us to preaching and teaching, as the Lord Jesus called the disciples from their nets. But, for the Christian, the work of preaching or the work of fishing are alike the Lord's work.

A LOW ENJOYMENT OF LIVING

We may rob ourselves of the joy of living in everything to His glory, if we bring only part of our lives under His sway. Children are notoriously practical in the delightful way in which they mention all sorts of trivial little things in their prayers. They naturally assume that God is concerned about every small detail of their lives. He Himself has told us that the very hairs of our heads are all numbered. 'Unless you . . . become like children . . .'

It is easy for us to become too intense in our effort to be 'as spiritual as possible'. I shall never forget a dear old missionary saying that one should pray to be both as spiritual as possible and as human as possible (in the proper sense). There should be no conflict between the two. In the Lord Jesus we find the most wonderful harmony of human and spiritual. We need not grudge time that must be given to household duties or family responsibilities as though they were less worthy occupations than others. We are to enjoy doing everything because we do it all to the glory of God. Many Christian

young people cut themselves off from all secular
society until they have very few friends outside their
small Christian circle, and the 'closed shop' type
of 'holy huddle' with no evangelistic outreach is the
result. There are students who join only the Christian Union and neglect other university societies
because they are 'secular'. If we can take part to
God's glory, then surely we should not hesitate to
join those in which we are interested and for which
we can find time. It is unfortunate if people can only
take part in normal, human activities with a sneak-
ing sense that they ought to be doing something
'more profitable'. We ought to be able to carry out
all our activities 'singing and making melody in
(y)our heart to the Lord; giving thanks always for
all things' (Eph. v.19, 20).

A PROPER PLACE FOR RECREATION

What of sport, games and other recreations? Are we
to classify these as unprofitable and unspiritual? It is
worth making some brief comment upon the value
and lawfulness of recreation. Christ mentions the
games of the children who play at weddings and
funerals. Paul does not hesitate to draw illustrations
from the games. Luke obviously enjoyed (and enjoyed reminiscing about) the cruising around the
Mediterranean incidental to their missionary work!
Paul, however, puts recreation in its proper place
when he tells Timothy: 'For while bodily training
is of some value, godliness is of value in every way'
(1 Tim. iv.8, RSV); i.e. it has its uses, but not of
course the same lasting, eternal value as exercise
unto godliness. Such bodily recreation may help to
keep us fit, for Him to use. For example, Fraser of

Lisuland used to take mountaineering holidays for recreation and relaxation. Later, as he worked in the mountains of S.W. China, this stood him in good stead: 'There had been unconscious preparation back in those Swiss summers, for the far more strenuous mountaineering that was to come. For in ways that often pass unnoticed God fits His instruments for the work He has in view.' [1]

It is not easy to find direct scriptural warrant for holidays and relaxation, though the principle of sabbath rest and the years of Jubilee seem to have some bearing upon this. Recreation is to the mind what sleep is to the body. An old traditional story of John the Evangelist relates that one day he was amusing himself with 'a tame partridge on his hand, when he was asked by a huntsman, how such a man as he could spend his time in so unprofitable a manner? To whom John replied, "Why dost thou not carry thy bow always bent?" "Because", answered the huntsman, "if it were always bent, I fear it would lose its spring and become useless." "Be not surprised, then," replied the apostle, "that I should sometimes remit a little of my close attention of spirit to enjoy a little recreation, that I may afterward employ myself more fervently in divine contemplation"!'

If our minds are to be used to the full, they must from time to time be rested and relaxed. Busy minds have not time for many recreations. Let such as are taken, then, be thoroughly refreshing. If our eating and drinking can be done to the glory of God, so also can our times of recreation and enjoyment be spent to His glory. As our lives get busier and our youthful

[1] Mrs Howard Taylor, *Behind the Ranges*, p. 20.

days draw to a close, our opportunity, and possibly our inclination, for violent physical exercise is diminished : we learn to relax while playing with children, walking in the country, enjoying natural history, digging in the garden, in the pleasure of some constructive hobby or of reading some absorbing topic away from our own particular work. We must beware of being obsessed by our recreations ; one may have far too much of a good thing. They can sometimes result in extravagant spending. But there is a real place in our lives for interests and employments which enable us to relax our tensions.

A TRUE INTEGRATION OF LIFE

This, then, is the sum of what we have been trying to say, that we need to see our lives as a unity, as an integrated whole devoted to God's glory. Paul prays for the young Christians in Colossæ, that they may live lives 'worthy of the Lord, fully pleasing to him, bearing fruit in every good work' (Col. i.10, RSV). We, too, are to be fruitful in *every good work*—in our business, in our homes, in church work, in our courting, in our married lives, in our parenthood, in our recreations and in our friendships. In all these things we want to live lovely and pleasant lives. The New Testament, as we shall see in later chapters, has much to say of the practical duties of wives and husbands, parents and children, management and labour, citizen and state. These things are in the Bible, as part of 'the whole counsel of God'. They matter. They all have a part to play in the doing of God's will on earth.

CHAPTER III

A DIVIDED MIND?

IF everything is to be one compartment, as we have suggested in the previous chapter, it raises certain practical difficulties. Does this mean that we must try and do two things at once, and that whenever we are doing anything we ought to have half of our mind occupied in thinking spiritual thoughts? The practical difficulties of doing this seem considerable, and really it seems to be the same old dichotomy under another guise. This is a division of thinking, rather than a division of allocation of time.

A second difficulty that arises is this. If we can practise the presence of God whatever we are doing, is it really necessary to set aside any times of special prayer or worship at all? If everything can be equally honouring to God, then it is as good to spend an hour playing tennis as it is to spend an hour in prayer, or an hour digging in the garden is as good as an hour spent in Bible study. But is this really so? If it is, then all the very challenging talks on sacrifice, urging us to give up activities we enjoy in favour of more profitable 'spiritual activities', have been rather wide of the mark.

PRIORITIES

The point that talks on sacrifice rightly make is that there are priorities in the Christian life which govern the particular activities which we fit into our daily programme. 'Seek ye first the kingdom of God, and his righteousness; and all these things shall be added unto you.' Whether Christians have always assessed rightly what the priorities are, is a different matter. The trouble often is that Christians assess their priorities by reference to accepted practice in the particular circles in which they move, rather than by reference to Scripture. We so easily follow the Christian crowd, and in doing so may accept distorted views of 'spirituality'. The great adventure of the Christian life is learning to be true to all the different principles found in Scripture, which never change, in all the differing circumstances of our daily lives, which are always changing. Our constant exercise is to see that we are true to Scripture rather than to tradition, however excellent. Scripture makes it plain that prayer must have an essential part in the Christian life—but it would not normally be right for the Christian to spend the whole day upon his knees. Recreation is a good thing—but it would not be right to spend *all* one's time playing tennis.

God in His providence has made our lives so that many and varied activities are necessary to the proper and full enjoyment of them. Scripture itself indicates certain essential ingredients for the balanced Christian life: time spent in the secret place alone with Him, reading the Scriptures to learn of Him, time spent in fellowship and worship and service with other believers. But, as we have said already, to these we must add those other activities which God has ordained—our work, our home relationships, our civic responsibilities and so on. These are also the Lord's work and are to be undertaken by us for Him. Our life is to be an integrated unity, a harmony of praise to God in every part. Of these many constituents which make up our lives, all of which can be done to the glory of God, some obviously have priority over others. It is not good to forsake essential duties for one's own pleasures, even if these can be done in a way which is pleasing to God. We grow in the Christian life as we learn to blend together all these different ingredients of living.

For example, it is better for a student to produce a really good essay which has to be handed in next day and not go to a religious meeting, than to attend the meeting at the cost of producing a skimped and unworthy effort. It would be best if he could have so organized his time that he was able to do both. It is better for a son to miss reading his Bible than for him to fail to help his mother with the shopping. The conflict would probably not have arisen, however, had he not been lazing in bed when he should have been reading his Bible. If he went to bed earlier and got up earlier, he could still have sufficient sleep and also fulfil both duties without any conflict. It is better that a father should be available at home, helping and playing with his children, than that he should spend every night of the week out at various meetings of one sort and another. We sometimes accept without thought some special and extraordinary occasion when the hero of some missionary biography is said to desert his responsibilities to his wife and family for years 'for the sake of the gospel', without realizing that one would need very special and extraordinary guidance to go against the general scriptural directions about duties to wife and children. Such an action, it seems to me, would be quite wrong and unbiblical unless there were clear guidance that some other higher principle overruled what Scripture normally enjoins.

First, then, let us sort out our priorities. We are not to grudge time spent on any lawful and expedient activity, but must learn to be fruitful in each particular good work and to worship and serve God in the doing of it.

THE PRACTICAL DIFFICULTY

It is easy enough to talk about doing everything to His glory; but most of us find that we go through many of the activities of the day without very much thought about the Lord for whom we are doing them. We read such a verse as: 'Whatsoever ye do in word or deed, do all in the name of the Lord Jesus' (Col. iii.17), and give mental assent to the excellence of such a way of going about things, while not really experiencing much of it in daily living. George Herbert may sing:

> All may of Thee partake;
>   Nothing can be so mean,
> Which, with this tincture, 'for Thy sake',
>   Will not grow bright and clean.
>
> A servant with this clause
>   Makes drudgery divine:
> Who sweeps a room, as for Thy laws,
>   Makes that and the action fine.

And we may sing it too. But when it actually comes to picking up the broom, it is often a very different story.

And yet the secret of true holiness would seem to be a habitual mindfulness and recollection of God's presence, or what is sometimes referred to as 'abiding' in Christ. It is said of the coming Messiah, in Isaiah xi.3, that He will be of 'quick understanding in the fear of the Lord', which may be more literally and beautifully translated 'He shall draw His breath in the fear of the Lord'. If only we could be like our Master in this. The same kind of idea seems to be suggested by the conjunction of phrases in Genesis xvii.1 where God says to Abram, 'I am the Almighty God; walk before me, and be thou perfect.' The secret of the upright walk is to realize that we live in the sight of God.

But does this mean that we are always to be thinking about God? That is perhaps not difficult when we are occupied with one of those things which requires no great amount of concentration, such as walking in the country, digging in the garden or working in the kitchen. Thus Brother Lawrence 'in the greatest hurry of business in the kitchen . . . still preserved his recollection and heavenly mindedness'.[1] But many of us are of human necessity engaged in studies and business which require our full mental concentration upon the particular matter in hand.

It is interesting to note here a letter written in 1801 by Henry Martyn, a brilliant young Cambridge mathematician, Senior Wrangler before his twentieth birthday, in which he says to his sister: 'For the labourer as he drives his plough, and the weaver as he works on his loom, may have his thoughts entirely disengaged from his work, and may think with advantage on any religious subject. But the nature of our studies requires such deep

---

[1] *The Practice of the Presence of God,* Fourth Conversation.

abstraction of mind from all other things as to render it completely incapable of anything else and that during many hours of the day.' One wonders whether the good ploughman and conscientious weaver could be as detached as Martyn suggests, but one appreciates his point. It seems, however, that he was wrong in feeling a conflict here. It was right that he should concentrate fully upon his studies, realizing that he was to please God *in his work*. Such undivided attention to our studies is essential to the proper fulfilling of them, and therefore it is a Christian duty to give ourselves wholeheartedly to them. Most of us, indeed, need to pray for more concentration that we may perform our work with real thoroughness, instead of doing it feverishly and hastily, with our attention distracted by thoughts of all the other things we shall have to be doing shortly. But by doing his work well, Martyn was doing it 'in the name of the Lord Jesus'. This is what the text means; it is done so well that the Lord would not be ashamed to call it His work.

Many of us would probably also echo the words that Martyn wrote in his journal after his Quiet Time: 'After my prayers my mind seems touched with humility and love, but the impression decays so soon.' This is a very common experience. If we do not begin the day rightly with prayer and Bible reading, we may expect to feel away from our Lord; but even when we have enjoyed a real sense of His presence at the start of the day, it is easy to feel spiritually stale and jaded after a morning spent in lectures, or dealing with difficult customers, or working with uncongenial companions.

GOD'S PROMISED PRESENCE

Part of the solution lies in realizing the danger of depending upon feelings as a sign of His promised presence. His presence is not dependent upon our consciousness of it. But there is more to it than this, for often we are conscious that we have insensibly lost contact with Him in all our rush and hurry. We have strayed from His side. This is all part of the frailty of our fallen human nature and the sinful world in which we live. We 'groan inwardly', as Paul puts it, and look forward to our final redemption from the very presence of sin when our walk and fellowship with Him may be unbroken. Yet none the less we must aim at a closer walk now with God. 'But is it then possible to realize the divine presence while engaged in exacting mental effort?' someone may ask, 'and, indeed, ought we to try to do so at all?'

What we need to develop is not the *feeling* of God's presence, but an awareness that He is present and that His eye is upon us. Such a consciousness need not be the same thing as deliberate recollection at all. One writer [1] says very helpfully that 'this consciousness need not interfere with the most active exercise of the powers of the mind, is clear from the following consideration: A man's mind is never more actively engaged than when he is making an extempore address . . . yet, what speaker for a moment forgets, or can forget, that the eyes of his audience are upon him? . . . It is clear that the consciousness of *a* presence need not interfere with the most active operations of the mind. And if con-

[1] E. M. Goulburn, *Thoughts on Personal Religion*, p. 174.

sciousness of the presence of man need not do so, why need the consciousness of the presence of God?' Such a speaker is rapidly doing a number of things with his mind : and yet at the same time he is conscious of his audience. He does not have to remind himself 'There are people here. There are people here.' He knows there are; indeed, he notes their reactions and is encouraged or discouraged by them. We need to pray that the Lord will give us such a deep sense of the reality of His presence, that we may learn to walk before Him and be perfect. All that I do, I do in the sight of God. I may think of His immanence, a God in whom we live and move and have our being (Acts xvii.28), or I may think of His indwelling through the Holy Spirit, or of the risen Lord Jesus at the right hand of God, as Stephen saw Him.

It is a great help if we can use the breaks and pauses in our work to lift our eyes to Him, to see if our actions and occupations are pleasing to Him. Nehemiah seems to have cultivated such an attitude, so that in one of his life's great crises we read, 'I prayed to the God of heaven. And I said unto the king . . .' (Ne. ii.4 f.). In time, we shall find that the constant lifting of our thoughts to God will pass into an instinctive and habitual resort to His presence whenever our mind is not entirely absorbed with necessary duties. Such is obviously only the result of diligent practice and persevering prayer. We need to begin every day with the prayer that we may 'lead a life worthy of the Lord, fully pleasing to him, bearing fruit in every good work and increasing in the knowledge of God' (Col. i.10, RSV), and we need to continue in that same frame of mind through all the business of the day. Such a mind is not one that we make blank in order to think of Him, but one that is increasingly conditioned to such thought by reading the Scriptures and obeying God's commands.

AN ORDERED LIFE

It is a thrilling thing to realize that as there is a sphere of glory prepared for us to occupy hereafter, so there is a sphere of good works prepared for us to occupy here. We are 'created in Christ Jesus unto good works, which God hath before ordained (prepared) that we should walk in them' (Eph. ii.10). What an adventure life becomes, when we realize that God has all sorts of things in store for us. One of the joys of being a Christian is that we may begin each day with a sense of pleasurable anticipation, wondering what adventures He has prepared for us.

> Father, I know that all my life
>   Is portioned out for me;
> The changes that will surely come
>   I do not fear to see;
> I ask Thee for a present mind
>   Intent on pleasing Thee.

Such an attitude will deliver us from all the fuss and bother, rush and hustle that we have come to think of as a life of Christian service. How often we think of the man engaged in such service as being one who rushes from one engagement to another, his pockets bulging with tracts, which he distributes in all directions as he goes; one who abounds with restless energy, but never has time to prepare any fresh talks, nor ever has time to spot the really needy individuals. Is this really the New Testament picture of what we are to aim at—a sort of evangelistic one man band? Compare this with the way the Lord Jesus lived. There was a time when He had no leisure so much as to eat; but somehow even then we never see Him hustled. For example, in Matthew ix, as soon as He reaches His own city a man sick of the palsy is brought to Him. He heals the man and makes the healing an occasion to display His power to forgive sins. Going out, He sees Matthew at his work and calls him to follow. Matthew obeys and invites Him to lunch at his house with his friends. The Lord accepts, and there He is able to speak of God's grace to sinners, and to explain why His disciples do not fast. Jairus arrives and calls Him to come to his daughter. Jesus sets off with him only to be interrupted by the woman with the issue of blood. Jairus' exasperated impatience at this delay is only too easy to imagine, but the Lord has time for this woman too, and then goes on to heal the little girl. On the way home the blind men call out to Him and are healed, and the man with the dumb spirit is brought to Him and is soon speaking. How wonderfully He moves quietly on from one thing to the next, getting so much done in the course of a day, without any sign of haste or worry. How different this is from the modern idea that the best Christian work is done by people who move at a near gallop, and who have to leave off at intervals for a nervous breakdown or peptic ulcer. It is the way in which we do things, rather than the tempo of our operations, which glorifies God. May we ask of the Lord Jesus:

Drop Thy still dews of quietness,
  Till all our strivings cease;
Take from our souls the strain and stress,
And let our ordered lives confess
  The beauty of Thy peace.

May we begin all our days with quiet expectancy, and praying 'Lord, enable me to walk in all the good works Thou hast prepared for me to walk in this day: and make me fruitful in every one of them.'

It is recorded of Enoch that he 'walked with God: and he was not; for God took him', and that he 'pleased God'. Campbell Morgan, commenting on Hebrews xi.5,[1] tells the delightful story of the little girl who 'went home from Sunday School after hearing the story of Enoch. She said : "Mother, we heard about a wonderful man today in Sunday School." The sensible mother let her child tell what she had heard. "His name was Enoch and you know, Mother, he used to go for walks with God." The mother said to her : "That is wonderful, dear. How did it end?" "Oh, Mother, one day they walked on and on, and got so far, God said to Enoch, You are a long way from home. You had better come in and stay with me." '

May our lives become one long wonderful walk with Him, until we are called to leave this sphere of good works to go to be for ever with Him.

Fill Thou my life, O Lord my God,
  In every part with praise,
That my whole being may proclaim
  Thy being and Thy ways.

[1] *Triumphs of Faith*, p. 46.

Not for the lip of praise alone,
  Nor e'en the praising heart,
I ask, but for a life made up
  Of praise in every part.

Praise in the common things of life,
  Its goings out and in;
Praise in each duty and each deed,
  However small and mean.

Fill every part of me with praise :
  Let all my being speak
Of Thee and of Thy love, O Lord,
  Poor though I be, and weak.

So shalt Thou, Lord, from me, e'en me,
  Receive the glory due;
And so shall I begin on earth
  The song for ever new.

So shall each fear, each fret, each care,
  Be turned into a song;
And every winding of the way
  The echo shall prolong.

So shall no part of day or night
  From sacredness be free;
But all my life, in every step,
  Be fellowship with Thee.

But such a wonderful life of praise is to be worked
out in the common things and in the common relationships of life. If Christians spent less time arguing
about the merits of various rival theories of sanctification, and more time discussing what sanctification
means in the details of daily living, it would do a
great deal more good. The following chapters attempt to make a few suggestions along such practical lines.

CHAPTER IV

FAMILY[1]

HUMAN life begins in the home. Thus it is no accident that in the Decalogue the command to 'honour thy father and thy mother' follows immediately after the four commandments which express our duty to God. It is the first of six commandments relating to our duty towards our neighbour. In the following chapters we shall consider each of these in turn. In each case we shall discover that the teaching of Scripture as a whole enlarges and enlightens our concept of all that God intends by each commandment. The scope of each is extended to cover one whole aspect of our lives, one in which, as we have already seen, we wish to be fruitful. The simple principle of the brief commandment has a very wide application. In this chapter we shall find that the fifth commandment covers the whole of our life in the home with our family.

It is in the home that our first training in obedience is received. The child will know the law of its parents before it knows the law of God. The Old Testament begins with a father and mother and their children. Indeed, its first book is all about parents and their children. The New Testament begins with the Lord Jesus being born into a home. We all start in the same way: we begin our lives in a home. It is not

---

[1] For a fuller treatment of the matters discussed in this chapter, see *Christian Witness in the Home*, by Major W. F. Batt (I.V.F.).

surprising, then, that Scripture has much to say to us about the home.

CHRIST IN THE HOME

If any son knew better than his parents, then surely the Lord Jesus did. If any young man had a right to be away about his father's business, then this One did. But we find that 'he went down with them, and came to Nazareth, and was subject unto them . . . and Jesus increased in wisdom and stature, and in favour with God and man' (Lk. ii. 51, 52). He obeyed and fulfilled the scriptural injunction to 'Honour thy father and thy mother'. If *He* did, then surely we must as well.

In His ministry we find Him time and time again in people's homes—in Simon Peter's, in Matthew's, in Jairus', in Zacchaeus', in Martha's—and always bringing joy and blessing with Him. A mother is healed, sinners befriended, a daughter restored, restitution made, a brother raised from the dead. It is significant that, frequently, it seems to be the first place to which He would be brought by a new disciple, as with Peter (Mk. i.29), Matthew and Zacchaeus. So Scripture underlines the fact that the first place where a changed life should be manifested is in the home. This is very striking in the case of the man called Legion who had been possessed by the devils (Lk. viii.39) and who wished to remain in our Lord's immediate retinue. He is told : 'Return to thine own house, and shew how great things God hath done unto thee.' The change wrought by his witness is suggested by the fact that, whereas at this time the people of Decapolis besought Christ to depart from them, when next He came that way, they 'bring unto him' one that was deaf. Their whole attitude seems to have changed, and the cause seems to have been the transformed life of the man who went home. 'Charity begins at home' has become a cliché which has lost its meaning, but many of us converted in our late teens have failed most miserably because we have been inconsistent at home and shown a lack of love towards our parents.

CHRISTIANS IN THE HOME

Do we spend sufficient time at home in the vacations, or do we treat our homes as a kind of free hotel to which we resort when there is nothing more interesting to do? And when we are at home, are we tucked away in our rooms reading or seeking our own enjoyment somewhere, when there is work to be done? How sad it is if our parents get the impression that they have outgrown their usefulness to us now that we are grown up. It is very easy to be so bound up with our own interests and our own friends, that we seem almost strangers to our parents, who long that they might still be able to enter into our joys and sorrows. In very strong terms Paul writes to Timothy: 'If any widow have children or (lit.) grandchildren, let them learn first to shew piety at home, and to requite their parents; for that is good and acceptable before God . . . if any provide not for his own, and specially for those of his own house, he hath denied the faith, and is worse than an infidel' (1 Tim. v. 4, 8). Our Lord Himself speaks in scathing terms of those who invoke some tradition to avoid this responsibility. It is noteworthy that the reason given to the parents was that 'what you would have gained from me is . . . given to God'—a

'spiritual' priority is pleaded (Mk. vii. 10–13, RSV).
As Christians we may fail in our duty to our parents
because we think that there is some religious reason
for it.

But surely this means more than to provide for the
physical needs of our own relations. If that were the
case, it would mean that if they were merely passed
on to the material care of some old people's home,
then we would have fulfilled our responsibilities. It
must mean the giving of time and loving interest and
sympathetic concern as well. Israel is reckoned as
decadent and worthy of judgment when 'Father and
mother are treated with contempt in you' (Ezk.
xxii.7, RSV). It is desperately easy to ignore aged
parents and treat them as tiresome children. Solomon counsels 'Hearken to your father who begot
you, and do not despise your mother when she is
old' (Pr. xxiii.22, RSV). We have a responsibility to
try, for our part, to share their interests and concerns,
and to seek to share ours with them.

WRITING HOME

And what of our letters home? Infrequent, short
and scrappy? Full of conventional commonplaces
which will fill up the page? Surely if we are to do all
things well for Him, then even our letter-writing
must be transformed. We shall give time to making
our letters as interesting and informative as possible,
remembering the things in which the family will be
particularly interested. Mothers, for example, are
often interested in personal details about clothing
which the average son hardly thinks twice about.
As people become older and feel increasingly out of
touch with the younger generation, the more our

letters can give pleasure and interest. When old people are unable to get out very much, then every letter from a child or grandchild is an event. It provides excitement and a topic of conversation for days! If our letters ended more frequently with a genuine expression of affection and less often 'in haste', it would be a real Christian witness. Many parents, never able to get to college or to have a holiday abroad themselves, and making sacrifices to send their own children, may yet enjoy it vicariously if the letters home are really interesting. It is a great thing if grandparents, parents and children can all share a mutual joy in each other: 'Grandchildren are the crown of the aged, and the glory of sons is their fathers' (Pr. xvii.6, RSV). How they love it when we do open our hearts to them and ask their counsel and advice! A father and son walking together in real companionship is a sight to bring joy to the heart. We must be ready to enter into the activities of our homes and not to be always preoccupied with our own affairs. While working on this chapter I was called to go and play Christmas games with the family. I could hardly refuse, could I?

The New Testament Epistles urge upon children and parents alike the duty of fulfilling their responsibilities (Eph. vi.1–4; Col. iii.20–21). Obedience to parents is seen to be pleasing to the Lord. Such obedience and deference is mentioned by Paul as part of the response of Christians to the gospel. Changed behaviour in the home is an intended result of redemption. This respect is to be extended to our elders generally—as, for example, other people's parents. Timothy, though in a position of ecclesiastical responsibility, is instructed to show respect to the 'elder' men and 'elder women' alike. Such deference will be shown by the tone used in conversation, by not dismissing their ideas as of necessity outmoded, and in such practical matters as opening doors, carrying bags and offering the more comfortable armchair to the visitor.

DIFFICULTIES IN THE HOME

If our parents are not Christians, we may find little response to, and understanding of, our new allegiance to Christ. It may be laughed at as a 'phase' or as a peculiarity. It is desperately difficult when there is a whole approach to life which our parents do not share. I once knew some parents who scoffed at their son's faith even in his later twenties, and who made his life a misery. He bore it all with long-suffering, gentleness and patience, so that his friends marvelled at the hardness of their hearts. It is all too easy to react in quite a different way, however. We just maintain a pitying tolerance : 'My parents are still pagan. They don't understand!' Friends are brought into our homes and we do not even have the courtesy to introduce them to our parents. We go about our own business without telling them where we are going or what we are doing, because we assume that, being non-Christians, they will have no interest. Perhaps they do not appear interested, but we owe it to them to try and share all that we can with them. It is only a new life, and a real display of love, which will convince sceptical parents that we really are different.

Our task may be made harder by possessive parents, mothers who still treat their children as infants, or who obviously hate the idea of their children marrying or leaving home. What grace the

Christian needs to show here! The Lord was subject, but the time came when He left home to fulfil His work. The time may come when, firmly and lovingly, we too may have to press on in face of parental possessiveness, remembering that 'If any man . . . hate not his father, and mother . . . he cannot be my disciple.' At the same time, let us never overlook the costly sacrifice on their part when they surrender us to the overseas mission cause, perhaps. It cannot have been easy for Hannah to part with her Samuel or for Lois and Eunice to see their Timothy travel away with Paul. A deep realization of that sacrifice and some expression of our love and appreciation may help them in their struggle with themselves at such a time.

PARENTHOOD

If you are a student, there is a high degree of probability that within ten years you will yourself be a parent. A diverting thought, no doubt! But this is a high office and dignity, and one for which we should prepare ourselves. It is a good thing to see something of small children and think out our ideas about bringing them up. In our reading of Scripture we shall note in passing many of the things that will be applicable when that day comes. The Old Testament gives many interesting illustrations of life in the home and the mistakes that are made. These things were written for our learning.

One thinks of the favouritism of Isaac for Esau, and Rebecca for Jacob, and the suspicion and deceit that resulted. When Jacob grew to manhood he too had his favourites—and Joseph was fast becoming a horribly spoilt child, a teller of tales and a boastful relater of dreams. Only the Lord's chastening produced in him the real fruits of godly character that he showed later. One notes the tenderness of Elkanah towards his disappointed wife Hannah, and her dedication of her son to the Lord. One contrasts Samuel with the ungodly sons of Eli, and his failure to control them, so that the Lord says that he honoured his sons more than God. We find Manoah and his wife (Jdg. xiii.8) praying, 'Oh my Lord, let the man of God which thou didst send come again unto us, and teach us what we shall do unto the child that shall be born', and then asking the 'man of God', 'How shall we order the child, and how shall we do unto him?' As we read the injunctions in the Proverbs, we shall pray that we may heed the warnings and imitate the examples. The writer well remembers the impression made on him in the early years after his conversion by visits to really Christian homes, and praying that the Lord might make him fit to have such a home. We need to prepare ourselves for homemaking.

There is another kind of preparation (see chapter vi) summed up in the story of the daughter who thanked her mother for 'choosing me such a nice Daddy'! To which her mother quietly replied, 'I hope your children will want to say the same to you!'

CHAPTER V

PEOPLE

ALTHOUGH it is our long-suffering parents who have to bear the brunt of our first entry into the world, it is not long before we begin to make an impact on a wider circle. The small boy soon learns that he is not the only boy in the world, and that he must live in a society full of other aggressive little boys. The sixth commandment thus has to do with our attitude to people in general, following our attitude to our parents in particular. In a fallen world the outcome of unrestrained competition between one man and another may well prove to be murder, as it was between Cain and Abel in the earliest days of the human race. 'Thou shalt not kill' embodies a recognition of human sinfulness and forbids men to live like animals on the principle of the survival of the fittest.

Human life is not to be taken with impunity. The Bible goes much further than this—human personality is sacred. It is sacred because God made man in His own image (Gn. ix.6). It is sacred because we must regard as of infinite value a man for whom Christ died (Rom. xiv.15). The human personality may also be sanctified by the indwelling Spirit of God, the Holy Spirit (1 Cor. vi.19). It is sacred because Christ Himself has for ever hallowed human personality by becoming man, being a partaker of flesh and blood, and not being ashamed to call us His brethren (Heb. ii.11 ff.). Because of this, far more is expected of the Christian believer than that he should simply refrain from murder. A new attitude of love towards men should be the positive outcome of our new relationship to God. The practical expression of this love is what is demonstrated in what we may call Christian courtesy. This courtesy is to be the subject of this chapter.

When our Lord expounds the sixth commandment in His sermon on the mount, He makes it quite plain that it is not only the outward act of murder that God forbids, but the inward attitude of hatred, the look of anger and the voice of scorn, 'Thou fool' (Mt. v.21 ff.). Later in the same chapter He indicates, in a more positive way, what our attitude should be. Far more is expected of the Christian than the return of kindness for kindness or the exchange of conventional greetings (Mt. v. 46, 47). In the Lucan version of the sermon this is even more forceful : 'If you love those who love you, what credit is that to you? For even sinners love those who love them. And if you do good to those who do good to you, what credit is that to you? For even sinners do the same' (Lk. vi. 32, 33, RSV). Like many so-called charities, which simply provide benefits for members and their dependants, this kind of benefaction is only a form of insurance : we give in order to get something in return. But, says our Lord, there is no grace in returning good for good, for then we give no more than we receive. What God looks for is that, like Him, we should give over and above that which might be expected of us, pressed down and running over. This is the basis of Christian courtesy.

Christian courtesy is more than common decency. God looks for uncommon decency ! Paul sums it up in his great section on love : 'Love is very patient, very kind. Love knows no jealousy; love makes no parade, gives itself no airs, is never rude, never selfish, never irritated, never resentful; love is never glad when others go wrong, love is gladdened by goodness, always slow to expose, always eager to believe the best, always hopeful, always patient. Love never disappears' (1 Cor. xiii.4–8, Moffatt). This is courtesy : not formality and politeness, but a genuine concern for, and a generous estimate of, other people. It involves a sensitivity to their scruples and the anticipation of their needs. We must be those who 'look for trouble', in the sense that we are always on the look out for any trouble that we can take for others. It is so easy to live our lives for our own advantage, our own enjoyment and to be forgetful of other people. The phrase 'seeketh not her own' (AV) always makes me remember an elderly don, a fine Christian and a very busy man indeed. In spite of all the claims on his time, nothing was too great a trouble for him to take for the most junior of students. Instead of sitting back and enjoying an aura of respect, he kept open house and constantly sought opportunities for doing personal kindnesses to his guests.

OTHER PEOPLE'S SCRUPLES

Love is kind; but Christians are often guilty of clumping over the scruples of others in hobnailed boots. It is in the context of other people's views that Paul says, 'Whether you eat or drink, or whatever you do, do all to the glory of God. Give no offence to Jews or to Greeks or to the church of God, just as I try to please all men in everything I do, not seeking my own advantage, but that of many, that they may be saved' (1 Cor. x.31–33, RSV). Here he mentions those whose views are different from ours because they belong to a different religion, or to a different culture, or even because there is freedom for differences within the Church in less important matters. If we have overseas guests, we shall be careful not to serve any form of pork for Jews or Muslims, or beef for Hindus. We may think their scruples peculiar, but it would be foolish to argue over such minor matters, when by winning their friendship we might be able to point them to the Lord Jesus. Christians are sometimes singularly tactless where non-Christians are concerned, in showing disapproval over matters of comparative indifference. If we are offered a cigarette, it is an act of generosity which we should appreciate. To reply that, in your opinion, it is a dirty, filthy habit, or even to say curtly, 'No, I don't smoke', may give offence. Non-Christian invitations to parties and entertainments must be treated courteously, even if refused.

In Romans xiv, where Paul treats of scruples in some detail, the examples that he gives concern the observing of days and seasons, and the question of abstention from food and drink. We may consider that others are far too strict about Sunday observance, or wrong to keep certain festivals. We may think them narrow in their attitude towards other issues. But it is wrong for us to grieve them in these things—and when we are their guests, and when we are in their company, we must respect their scruples. We are also told not to judge those who, we think, are not as definite about some of these matters as we would be.

Within the Church, again, many a careless or even deliberately provocative statement by an Anglican may deeply wound a Nonconformist (Free Churchman is a more courteous expression!) and vice versa. Our jokes about other people's denominations often seem funnier to us than they do to them, and not infrequently spring from ill-concealed pride in our own denomination and a shocking ignorance of the beliefs and practices of other churches. Even an elementary knowledge of English Church history, and the reasons for the separation of different groups, would help to remedy this. Free Churchmen are often guilty of dismissing the whole of the Established Church as being rotten with formalism and superstition, while Anglicans may scornfully lump orthodox Christian Churches with the 'sects'. How foolishly and dishonourably Christians sometimes talk, and how shameful is the ignorance that we reveal, and how we give offence to the Church of God!

OTHER PEOPLE'S BACKGROUNDS

One of the wonderful things about the Christian Church is the way in which people from many different backgrounds are welded together into one fellowship. One thinks of the converts in Philippi— a wealthy cultured business-woman like Lydia, a slave girl and a rough gaoler—all so very different in their backgrounds. In Colossians iii.11 Paul rejoices that in Christ 'there is neither Greek nor Jew, circumcision nor uncircumcision, Barbarian, Scythian, bond nor free: but Christ is all, and in all'. All Christians have Christ's presence within them through His indwelling Spirit, and if we have Christ, then we have all that we need. This was a necessary reminder in a letter to Colossae, where a false idea of a spiritual hierarchy having special doctrines not to be shared with the uninitiated *hoi polloi* had crept into the church. The barbarians were those ignorant people who could not speak Greek, and Scythians were the most boorish and uncouth of all barbarians, but in Christ there is to be no such cultural or racial snobbery. It is very easy for the university student to give the impression of feeling superior to those who are less fortunate, and who perhaps drop an occasional aitch. There is, however, no place in the Christian Church for this or for upholding the alleged superiority of Oxbridge over Redbrick universities (architecturally, Keele has some advantage over Keble!), or of the monastic boarding-school over the co-educational day-school. We must beware of superficial judgments of other Christians based upon their mode of dress, manner of speech, old school tie, university or family background. It is even possible for us to despise Christian movements that we may consider less enlightened than our own. There are cults of personality and cults of doctrinal emphasis in Christian circles which lay us open to another type of unbiblical 'puffed-up-ness'. Love is not puffed up. Let us learn from the changed attitude of the once proud Pharisee, graduate of Tarsus, Hebrew of Hebrews, Roman citizen, who might well have gloried in all this, yet who is happy to call the worthless runaway slave Onesimus a 'brother beloved, specially to me'.

We can often be unintentionally discourteous when we meet an old school or college friend, in the presence of some third person who does not share the same common background. Such a person may feel quite left out while we enjoy a good gossip about old times. If we have been to a university and they have not, then they are often sensitive to what they feel is our superior attitude. It is only good manners to change the conversation so that they are able to join in. The same principle holds good for other subjects of conversation, such as mutual acquaintances: if the third party doesn't know 'old So-and-So' then he will feel left out.

OTHER PEOPLE'S SENSITIVITIES

People are sensitive about many things—ill health, physical deformity, anatomical peculiarities and so on. It is very offensive to be boisterously healthy in front of a sick person, or to enthuse about games that they have never been able to play. We need to be especially courteous to those who have any deformity, treating them in a perfectly natural manner and yet being ready to help in an unostentatious fashion with anything they are not able to do for themselves, without making them feel less independent.

It is not kind to make jokes about people who may be rather small, or fat or tall or ungainly. Nor is it good enough to excuse ourselves by saying that they are prepared to laugh at themselves, for many a sensitive person would do anything rather than show how much he or she dislikes such personal remarks. It is an easy type of humour to slip into, and we need to be sure that we are not causing hurt when we make such remarks. It is also very easy to ignore some people who are quiet and apparently dull and unattractive; we would so much rather talk to the attractive people. Yet how many there are who must pine for that bit of interest and attention which we should make it our delight to give.

People from overseas may feel very unfamiliar with our customs, afraid of making some mistake, and unable to understand very well the long words that we use quite naturally. We must therefore do all that we can to make them feel at home. Often they may think that we are far more conscious of colour differences than in fact we are, and we want to put them at their ease by treating them just like anybody else. Overseas students loathe anything which seems at all patronizing. We are often appallingly ignorant of the great material progress made in many overseas countries, and speak as though these people were savages just emerged from the bush, or treat them as we might a rather large and dangerous kind of child. Overseas visitors are quick to sense anything unnatural in our behaviour towards them.

OTHER PEOPLE'S NEEDS

In the parable of the sheep and goats our Lord says, 'I was an hungred, and ye gave *me* meat : I was thirsty, and ye gave *me* drink : I was a stranger, and ye took *me* in. . . . Inasmuch as ye have done it unto one of the least of these my brethren, ye have done it unto *me*' (Mt. xxv.35–40). In every one of our brethren we may see the Lord Jesus, so that, in a sense, even the smallest kindnesses which we do them we are doing to Him. When we withhold a kindness, then we withhold it from Him. Human personality is as sacred to God as that. James tells us that pure religion involves visiting the fatherless and widows in their affliction. One can give a great deal of pleasure to lonely people by spending time with them. Paul gratefully remembers Onesiphorus, who 'oft refreshed me, and was not ashamed of my chain : but, when he was in Rome, he sought me out very diligently, and found me' (2 Tim. i. 16, 17). He obviously took real trouble to find Paul. In a strange city we are often able to renew our contacts with old friends, and perhaps lonely widows and other elderly relatives. A good cheerful visit to someone who is sick in hospital helps to relieve the tedium of the long day, and shows that we have not forgotten them, and care enough to come and see them. I heard of a lady once who used to ask the local hospital to tell her of any who had no visitors, and then used to go and visit them. Surely it is well-pleasing to God when we thus meet the needs of others.

OTHER PEOPLE AS INDIVIDUALS

I wonder whether you have ever noticed that all the stories that we so love in the Gospels are about individuals. Even when the story is that of the feeding of the five thousand, the lad with the five loaves and two fishes is the starting-point. Our Lord always has time for them; for Nicodemus, for the woman of Samaria, and so many others. Even when the crowds throng Him and He is on His way to the house of an important personage, He yet has time for the woman with the issue of blood. It is so easy for us to forget that groups of people are made up of persons, all with their own gifts and their own problems. It is so easy to treat human beings almost as machines, fulfilling a certain function : the woman who cleans the stairs, the man at the counter, the bus driver.

Individuals can become cases, such as 'the appendix in the fifth bed along'.

When we read the Epistle to the Romans, we often skip over the last chapter of greetings and fail to notice how remarkable it is that, though Paul had not so far been to Rome, he appends the longest list of personal greetings found in any of his Epistles. He has somehow kept track of the Christians he has met and knows their whereabouts and present circumstances. One may imagine him meeting a friend from a city where he had been, and asking for example : 'And where is Epaenetus now? In Rome? Then I may perhaps meet him there one of these days.' How pleased the Christians in Rome must have been when so many of them found that he had not forgotten them, and knew where they were. He showed a real concern for people and a real interest in them. It is an act of courtesy to try and remember people's names whenever we possibly can. If we find remembering names difficult, then let us be practical and write down their names after we have left them, and then make a point of addressing them by name next time we see them. Remembering names and little details about the people who answer to them is one way of pleasing all men in everything we do.

OTHER PEOPLE'S TIME

Most Christians recognize the need to be good stewards of their own time, but in so doing often make it very difficult for others to discipline theirs. Lack of punctuality is very common among Christians. If we arrive late for some appointment or for a meeting, then we have wasted other people's time, as well as breaking our word about the time when we promised to arrive. We may have saved five minutes for ourselves, but if we have kept a dozen people waiting for us, then an hour of Christian time has been wasted. As often as not our late arrival is a selfish failure to put other people's convenience before our own. We see it as 'just finishing off something I wanted to do', but what this really means is, 'I want to do something, and everyone else can wait for me.' If we know that we may be late because of the times of trains or a traffic hold-up, then it is courteous to warn others that we may not arrive on time, so that they do not delay on our account. We can be punctual when we really want to be; appointments with drill sergeants on the one hand and fiancées on the other are strictly kept. If we arrive late at church services or at lectures, our entry may be a cause of distraction and disturbance to others. Sometimes our lateness is unavoidable, but more often it is because we have failed to plan our time properly, and because we have thought only of our own convenience.

Interruptions are often very irritating, but to go on reading and ignore the newcomer, or to pretend that we really are too busy just now, and to keep people cooling their heels just to impress them with the fact, is most discourteous and again springs from the selfish notion that the only person who really matters is *me*. Consideration for others also involves thought about whether the time at which we interrupt others is convenient for them. To arrive too early or too late or at a mealtime is always discourteous.

OTHER PEOPLE'S LETTERS

Other people's letters are the ones we have written the previous day! We ourselves always enjoy an interesting letter, and it is worth taking the trouble to write a letter which will give real pleasure to the one who receives it. 'We always enjoy getting your letters' is a testimony that every Christian should aim at. So often our letters are terse, vague and full of inadequately expressed ideas, and obviously written in a tearing hurry. It is as rude to write such a letter as it would be to speak to someone in the same sort of way. Now and again we are boiling to write some scalding letter of protest or criticism, but we need to cool down and try to see the other person's approach, so that we may finally write a gracious and tactful letter which fulfils the injunction to 'give none offence'. It seems a shame that all too often the only long and potently expressed letters we write are angry ones.

It is also worth adding that letters received demand a reply. It used to be said of one Christian man that, if you really wanted a reply, you had to send a telegram, and of another that you had to write to his wife! Contrast the readiness with which people interrupt anything to answer the telephone, with the readiness with which they find a hundred and one things to do rather than answer a letter. If we cannot give a definite reply at once, then it is only courteous to write and say so in a brief acknowledgment.

A well-known Christian minister in London, who is invited to speak at far more meetings than he is ever able to attend, spends some twenty pounds a year sending courteous refusals to people who discourteously forget to enclose stamped addressed envelopes. To enclose a stamped addressed envelope is the least we can do when we expect a reply from busy people.

OTHER PEOPLE'S HOMES

When we are invited to stay with people, it is only considerate to drop them a card telling them when we hope to arrive and by what route we expect to be travelling. Otherwise our poor hostess may spend hours trying to keep a meal ready for whatever time we may arrive, and is unable to go out lest we arrive and find the house empty. If we have stayed for the night or been given a major meal then a 'bread-and-butter' letter is called for, and we should put honey on it, too. They have put themselves out for us, and taken on extra bedmaking, cooking and cleaning: let us not be chary of expressing our real gratitude for all their kindness. It must be a very rare circumstance when we cannot find anything to pay a compliment about. When we are there, let us give all the help we can : many people seem to think it polite to refuse our first offer of help, so let us persevere. We ought not to presume on the hospitality of others or to overstay our welcome. We may be enjoying a good chat, but do they normally stay up this late, I wonder? Remember the sound piece of advice : 'Withdraw thy foot from thy neighbour's house; lest he be weary of thee' ! (Pr. xxv.17). It is far better to leave early and then be wanted back again, than to stay on and on till hints have to be dropped. Remember the dreadful fate of the Rev. Melpomenus Jones who called for tea and stayed for six weeks: ' "Well I think I . . ." But the lady of the house said : "Oh, no ! Mr Jones, can't you really stay a little longer ?" Jones was always truthful, "Oh, yes," he said, "of course, I—er—can stay." "Then please don't go." He stayed. He drank eleven cups of tea. Night was falling. He rose again. "Well now," he said shyly, "I think I really . . ." ' But he finally allowed himself to be prevailed upon to stay the night, and the following day, and so on for six weeks.[1]

Courtesy in using the bathroom and bedroom is also important. It is courteous to discover at what time it is convenient for us to use the bathroom, and then we avoid the rather embarrassing situation in which we keep everyone else out of it at the most awkward time. In these days, too, it helps the busy housewife if we strip our own beds before we leave, clean the bath after using it and help with the washing-up.

Most households are enlivened with children, and as Christians we shall not ignore them, but treat them as personalities in their own right. What a delight children can be, but how careful we must be not to make them show off. We sometimes cause offence because we treat children in a way which is childish, and fail to pay due regard to their age and interests. If we can discover their interests and enthusiasms, it will prevent them being snowed under with the usual grown-up enquiries about how they are getting on at school ! We must also be especially careful not to interfere with the way in which their parents are trying to bring them up.

[1] Stephen Leacock, *Literary Lapses*, Penguin edition.

EMPLOYERS AND SERVANTS

Scripture is full of injunctions about the relations between what we would, today, call management and labour. A certain amount has already been said in the introductory chapters about our attitude to work. Obedience, submission and respect are commanded, irrespective of the kindness or harshness of the employer. As students, this obedience and respect is due to members of university staff as those from whom we are to learn. Students sometimes trade on the friendship of senior Christians, and fail to treat them with sufficient deference. There is sometimes too great a familiarity with guest speakers—one distinguished speaker remarked upon the freedom with which hitherto unknown Christian students addressed him by his Christian name within a few minutes of introduction. There is nothing about one's fellowship with Christians which obviates the use of the customary respectful 'Sir' when we address sympathetic members of university staff.

We should always show a proper respect for those older than ourselves and make a point of addressing them correctly. Young Christians often fail here in their chairing of meetings. 'The Rev. W. H. Jones' is correct on an envelope or a notice, but he should be introduced as 'Mr Jones' and never, as one so often hears, as 'Rev. Jones'. To introduced abbreviated names, such as 'Bill Jones', is equally discourteous.

We also need to be courteous to those who do work for us: our college cooks or cleaners, lab. assistants, etc., and to those who serve us in other ways, like shopkeepers and landladies. Some Chris-

tians in rooms have been much loved by their landladies for their kindness and considerateness. Non-
Christians so often treat those who serve them in
college as being quite unworthy of their notice, and
we must, therefore, see that our attitude does not
appear in any way patronizing, but rather shows our
real appreciation of their service. One senior porter
of a Students' Union, who was an old friend from
college days, told me that when anyone said 'Please'
or 'Thank you' through the enquiry hatch at the
porters' lodge, they looked up to see who it was. A
Christian can also witness in a very real way by his
friendliness towards those who serve in shops, or who
supply his needs in any other capacity.

OTHER PEOPLE ON THE ROAD

The peculiar change in behaviour which overcame
Toad of Toad Hall whenever he sat at the wheel of a
car is something to which even we Christians are not
altogether immune. All too often the driver seems to
cast aside his normal standards of courtesy when on
the road, and the old rule of every man for himself
seems to exert a far stronger influence upon him than
usual. Somehow the machine becomes more important than the other man, especially when we have
allowed just that little bit less time to get from A to
B than it normally takes. Here the Christian should
take especial care, for very often he is quite as busy
as (if not busier than) the next man, but he has also
to obey the injunction 'Thou shalt not kill', and that
little bit of extra speed, that risk taken by overtaking
when there is not quite enough time to do it com-
fortably, or by shooting the lights, may cost some
innocent person his life. To speed, or to overtake at

the possible risk of life, is therefore forbidden to the Christian according to God's law.

In addition to this, a lack of courtesy on the roads is a failure on the part of the Christian to make use of this real opportunity to witness to his Master. We may not see the need to keep to the thirty-mile-an-hour limit when the road ahead seems reasonably clear, but these laws are made for our good and if we, as Christians, break the law just as other men do, then we are failing to show the difference that knowing Christ makes in these seeming trivialities of everyday life. Nor is the Christian likely to please God by losing his temper and shouting or blaring his horn when he considers another driver has done something foolish, or is holding him up. As in every sphere of human activity, our driving may be done to the glory of God, or we may grieve Him by our careless and discourteous behaviour.

OTHER PEOPLE AT CLOSE QUARTERS

Many people today share rooms or lodgings, and relations between room-mates are often extraordinarily bad. This is especially the case when they are very different in temperament and habits : as when one is very tidy and the other chaotic, or one goes to bed early and the other works into the small hours, when one likes jazz and the other classical music. The smallest and the silliest things can often become causes of friction. Sadly, this may even happen when one of the parties is a Christian. It does need a very real measure of grace to get on with another person, especially when you have had no say in choosing whom you share with, but have just been put with someone else. One person empties the milk bottle or

the box of matches, and leaves the other to find
them empty and replenish the supply.

Yet in the mercy of God more people seem to
have been brought to Christ through having to share
with a Christian than in almost any other way. At
Trinity College, Dublin one may be rather startled
to find another fellow introduced as 'my wife' until
one appreciates that this is the traditional term for
the 'room-mate' of other colleges. Probably only in
married life does one have to share rooms with
another person so intimately, and then one is able to
choose. But sharing rooms can help us to see how
selfish we have been getting, just doing what we
liked when we liked, without having to consult anyone else's convenience.

This chapter has included many practical and
apparently trivial points, but it is in things such as
these that we are to show forth the love of Christ to
others.

CHAPTER VI

SEX

CONCERNING our relations with other people, much that we have said already may be given a general application, but the existence of two sexes provides further complications. If I were the only boy in the world, and she were the only girl, the problems would be considerably simplified. Under such circumstances the plain statement of the Decalogue : 'Thou shalt not commit adultery' would be unnecessary. But because we live in a more complex society, such a prohibition is needed, together with the fuller exposition of God's will that we find in the New Testament in the teaching of Christ and His disciples. Many otherwise consistent and consecrated Christians fail miserably at this point. A person's witness is spoilt, or his own devotional life hindered, because of inconsistency in his relations with the other sex.

It is not the purpose of this chapter to trespass on the ground which has been so well covered in *Towards Christian Marriage.*[1] That volume, however, is often read in a special rosy context of its own, and often with one particular person in mind, so that there does seem to be a place in a discussion of Christian behaviour for a more general treatment of our attitude towards the opposite sex.

---

[1] Previously published under the title *Heirs Together*, by W. Melville Capper and H. Morgan Williams (I.V.F.).

IRRESPONSIBLE ATTITUDES

It is very easy for us to be subtly influenced in our thinking about sex by the views that have been current in the world around us from our earliest days. Few people can have been brought up in a place where they have been entirely sheltered from the distorted and degraded ideas of sex which are disseminated by magazines, books, wireless, films and television. Many schools now give a form of sex education which describes marriage largely in physical terms. Some literature seems to be based on the view that sex is given for the selfish satisfaction of our instincts. Other literature and entertainment of a more wholesome kind is still distorted when it gives the impression that it is all a matter of emotional fulfilment and romanticism. These views are inadequate, because they separate personal enjoyment of sex from personal responsibility. We need to be constantly on our guard against these inadequate mechanical and sentimental views of 'love' which are so much a feature of modern western society. God has endowed sexual fulfilment with joy and pleasure, but the privilege is meant to go with the responsibility of caring for wife and children. Such views are a real danger to marriage if they magnify the physical element beyond the place which it can legitimately occupy in marriage. Essentially, marriage is a friendship and companionship which is greatly deepened, and given its unique character by the physical relationship, and by the fact that it normally involves the privileges and labour of bringing up children.

A FALSE PRUDISHNESS

There is a danger that we may react against this undue emphasis on the physical, and adopt the equally unchristian idea that this great gift of God is in some way defiled and unworthy. We would then believe celibacy to be the true way of holiness, and marriage a second best. Christians of a former generation have said that in their youth they were distinctly given the impression that marriage was 'of the flesh', one of the necessary evils of this life. Such a reaction against the false ideas current outside the Church is still, unfortunately, all too common. We therefore need to reorientate our thinking by constant reference to the sane common sense of Scripture, as we navigate between the Scylla of a debased sensuality and the Charybdis of an unbiblical prudishness.

For the Bible declares that 'Marriage is honourable in all, and the bed undefiled' (Heb. xiii.4). The view that matter is sinful, and that everything physical is defiled and 'unspiritual', is pagan and not Christian. It is in the context of those who forbid marriage that Paul says that 'every creature of God is good, and nothing to be refused, if it be received with thanksgiving'. He even seems to suggest that these things were given by God for the special enjoyment of those 'which believe and know the truth' (1 Tim. iv.3–5). There is no prudishness in the proverb about a man's rejoicing in his wife (Pr. v.19), nor in the details of the Song of Solomon. The inclusion of this in the sacred canon—spiritualize it how you will—surely suggests that this is a worthy field of illustration. The Christian is to be fruitful in every good work and this includes a whole-hearted and unprudish approach to sex.

It is, I think, worth while to get this general attitude sorted out before going on to deal with our everyday contacts with the opposite sex. It is because Christians have often failed to think out their positions along the lines indicated, that there has been a failure on the part of otherwise consistent Christians to be gracious and courteous in these relations.

AN UNFORTUNATE SELF-CONSCIOUSNESS

A friend of mine, after a year spent overseas, commented on the young women of a certain great country : 'They look on every eligible young man as a potential mate. Even the Christian girls seem to have the attitude : "I wonder whether this is the one?"' He found it all very embarrassing. Such an attitude on the part of men or women cannot but make for very strained relationships between the sexes. If we are constantly on the look out for a life partner in this way, it will make for a very difficult atmosphere. There have been situations in our own country where a young woman has taken an invitation out to tea as tantamount to a proposal of marriage. Everybody is so self-conscious, even about speaking to a member of the opposite sex. Fearful of their good manners being mistaken for advances, men have behaved almost boorishly, failing in such normal courtesies as acknowledging ladies in the street, opening doors for them or speaking pleasantly to newcomers or someone sitting next to them. Timothy is told to treat the younger women as sisters, with all purity. Phillips paraphrases this as 'Treat the younger women as sisters, and no more' (1 Tim. v.2). That's it. We are to recognize that members of the opposite sex should receive our courteous consideration, as sisters (or brothers) but nothing more. After all 99·9999% of the members of the opposite sex whom we meet will never be our life partners, and can be treated in a perfectly normal, friendly way, without any nonsense. A little more common sense and a great deal less romantic imagination would make for far less of this self-consciousness.

PURE IN THOUGHT

In the sermon on the mount our Lord plainly states that lusting by looking is in fact committing adultery in the heart. 'Wherewithal shall a young man cleanse his way?' asks the Psalmist, and we realize again how alert and how relevant the Bible is to the problems and temptations which are common to all of us. 'By taking heed thereto according to thy word' is the answer given. It requires both effort and reference to the teaching of Scripture if we are to 'cleanse our way'. Many seem to carry over into adulthood a form of romantic dreaming begun in childhood which becomes increasingly sexual in content.

In these days there are many things to read, hear and see which will encourage us in wrong and impure thinking. Discipline is all the harder in times of idleness, as poor David found, and if the mind is allowed to dwell on impure imaginations at such times we are only predisposing it to weakness. The author still bitterly regrets that in moments of boredom in the Forces, he allowed himself to read litera-

ture left lying around by others. It leaves a bitter
taste in one's mouth and a contaminated place in
one's thinking. 'Flee . . . youthful lusts' says Paul to
Timothy (2 Tim. ii.22) and that is the only remedy;
get away from sources of temptation, as Joseph fled
from the temptation that he met. In the context of
His words about adultery, our Lord speaks of pluck-
ing out the eye and cutting off the hand that causes
us to offend. A radical treatment is needed. We must
learn to lay aside the novel which benefits us nothing
but only smirches the thoughts. We must learn to
switch off the radio or television play which has low
standards. We must learn to break off associations
which would hinder our pure thinking. There is a
real place for radical treatment—cutting out all that
infects and poisons.

On the positive side we need to fill our mind with
good and excellent ideas, 'Whatsoever things are
pure, whatsoever things are lovely, whatsoever things
are of good report . . . think on these things' (Phil.
iv.8). We find an instructive illustration of such positive filling of the mind in Henry Martyn's journal,
shortly before he sailed for India.

'*May* 30. Went to India House. Kept the covenant with my eyes pretty well. Oh, what bitter experience have I had to teach me carefulness against
temptation. I have found this method, which I have
sometimes had recourse to, useful today, namely—
that of praying in ejaculations for any particular
person whose appearance might prove an occasion
of sinful thoughts. After asking of God that she
might be as pure and beautiful in her mind and
heart as in body, and be a temple of the Holy Ghost,

consecrated to the service of God, for whose glory she was made, I dare not harbour a thought of the opposite tendency.'[1]

We need to keep our minds pure for Him, and for the life partner to whom He may bring us in His own time.

PURE IN DEED

We must have a very deep respect for the sacredness of human personality and determine to say or do nothing which would wound or hurt another. We need to pray that we may be kept from hasty or precipitate action; for, as young people, it is easy for us to act, not so much wilfully, as foolishly, in a way which we shall later regret. It is selfish and thoughtless to act on the impulse of the moment in initiating a deeper friendship, if we have failed to pray and think it over carefully. Let us ask ourselves: Have we prayed, and have we really thought about it, so that we are ready to see this through to the end?

Many of us are excited at the very thought of loving and being loved, and may rush precipitately into an emotional friendship for the love of being loved, rather than because of a real deep love for the other person. The cruel injury done by Amnon to Tamar (2 Sa. xiii) shows how a purely physical attraction may result in disaster for both parties. 'The hatred wherewith he hated her was greater than the love wherewith he had loved her.' His physical passion turned into revulsion. And she 'went on crying' and 'remained desolate in her brother Absalom's house'. These things were written for our learning.

[1] Smith, *Henry Martyn*, p. 77.

REJOICE WITH THEM THAT DO REJOICE

We need to be careful that our blessings do not become a curse to others. Perhaps some of our friends have had an inner battle over willingness to remain single, or over a disappointed friendship. It is not kind to be too affectionate either in word or gesture to your own beloved in front of others who are not similarly blessed. Some public demonstrativeness is more than embarrassing to others; it can be a cause of stumbling. Even Christians can be terribly insensitive in this matter. Not long ago I heard a Christian man extolling the blessedness of matrimony in front of rows of single women who had surrendered their hopes of a home and marriage to serve their Lord on the foreign mission field. The married could rejoice with him, but the unmarried could not. It was only thoughtlessness, but it was very hurtful. Young people can often be very unkind in ragging older persons about their single state. Perhaps they would have chosen otherwise, perhaps there is a deep scar hidden there; so let us think more about others before we indulge our clumsy, foolish humour. With those who are married or engaged, of course, we can rejoice quite freely, but let us beware lest we cause unnecessary pain when in mixed company.

KIND IN DEED

Peter tells husbands to give honour to their wives 'as unto the weaker vessel' (1 Pet. iii.7) and this principle surely extends to the way in which we treat any woman. Paul tells Timothy to treat 'the elder women as mothers; the younger as sisters, with all purity. Honour widows that are widows indeed' (1 Tim.

v.2, 3). This recognition of the woman as the weaker
vessel is the essential reason for offering a seat in a
bus or train, or for offering to carry some heavy case
or bag. Similarly, standing up when a lady comes
into a room allows her to choose the most comfortable chair. Such courtesies are not outdated customs,
but are ways in which we can show that honour
which Scripture enjoins.

CHAPTER VII

THINGS

FROM our consideration of the Christian attitude towards people, we now turn to consider our attitude towards things, be they animate or inanimate. 'Thou shalt not steal' is a commandment about possessions and is an expression of the extreme to which a wrong attitude to things will lead us. At first sight it appears that our Lord does not expound this in the sermon on the mount as He does the sixth and seventh commandments. On a closer look, however, we see that while this commandment is not explicitly referred to, we are given, in Matthew vi, a great revelation of the mind of God concerning the attitude of His creatures towards material things.

As always, our Lord is concerned with the attitude of the heart. One may commit murder in the heart and one may commit adultery in the heart; and 'where your treasure is, there will your heart be also'. The trouble about possessions is that they compel our constant care and anxiety. On earth they have to be constantly protected and insured against theft, and guarded from the attack of natural forces. Moths eat our clothes, white ants our houses, woodworm our furniture, booklice our libraries, damp and corrosion our cars and bicycles. Fire, flood and tempest still render many homeless every year. As Christians our treasure is to be with God, in whom is all our trust. We are not to be in a state of worldly care and anxiety about food and drink and clothing. Yet we live in a world in which mankind in general lives for material things : for property, mink coats, motor cars, good food and drink. It is no exaggeration to apply the words of the apostle, they 'worshipped and served the creature more than the Creator' (Rom. i.25), to modern society. People do worship and serve things; all their effort is concentrated on getting more things and keeping them. They live for them; they have nothing else to live for.

It is very easy for the Christian to be tainted with this anxious attitude about material provision for his future : to be always worrying about whether he will be able to make ends meet. Our Lord reminds us that the heavenly Father, who has given us life, can also provide the means to support life, just as He feeds the birds of the air, and clothes the lilies of the field. We must get this into proper perspective, 'for after *all these things* do the Gentiles seek'; but the children of God are meant to live differently. Our first great aim, our number one priority, is to seek the kingdom of God and His righteousness. But our Lord adds, if you do this, if you put Him absolutely first, then '*all these things* shall be added unto you'. There is nothing intrinsically wrong with all these things, but they are to be received as a by-product of serving God and not to be desired for their own sake. It is the same principle as that which operates when we are told that if we seek to keep our lives for ourselves, then we shall lose them; but if we are willing to lose our lives for His sake, then we shall save them. All these things will be added to us if we put first things first. We shall enjoy them. Things are not gods to which we give worship, but the gifts of the God whom we worship.

A POSITIVE ATTITUDE TO THINGS

What, then, is the scriptural teaching about things? Speaking of some who will depart from the faith in later days, 'forbidding to marry, and commanding to abstain from meats, which God hath created to be received with thanksgiving of them which believe and know the truth', Paul enunciates the general principle 'for every creature of God is good, and nothing to be refused, if it be received with thanksgiving : for it is sanctified by the word of God and prayer' (1 Tim. iv.3–5). This passage even seems to suggest that for the Christian there is a deeper measure of joy in these things because he believes and knows the truth of God the great Giver. Thus, things are not some kind of 'booby trap' which God has set to bring judgment upon our heads, but precious gifts to be enjoyed.

Calvin reminds us that God in His providence created things for our good, and continues : 'If we consider for what end He created food, we shall find that He consulted not only for our necessity, but also for our enjoyment and delight. Thus in our clothing the end was, in addition to necessity, a comeliness and honour; and in herbs, fruits and trees besides their various uses, gracefulness of appearance and sweetness of smell. Were it not the prophet would not enumerate among the mercies of God "wine that maketh glad the heart of man, and oil to make his face to shine" (Ps. civ.15). The Scriptures would not everywhere mention in commendation of His benignity, that He had given such things to men. The natural qualities of things themselves demonstrate to what end and how far they may be lawfully enjoyed. Has the Lord adorned flowers with all the beauty which spontaneously presents it to the eye, and the sweet odour which delights the sense of smell, and shall it be unlawful for us to enjoy this beauty and this odour? What? Has He not so distinguished colours as to make some more agreeable than others?' (*Inst*. III. x.2).

The Psalmist, as Calvin reminds us, sees a great deal of 'God's glory and grace' in natural providence and we should be wrong to let 'the things of earth grow strangely dim', if in them God expects us to see something of that glory of God which the heavens declare. It is just because God has provided 'the grass to grow for the cattle, and herb for the service of man: that he may bring forth food out of the earth; and wine that maketh glad the heart of man, and oil to make his face to shine, and bread which strengtheneth man's heart', that the Psalmist sings 'O Lord, how manifold are thy works! in wisdom hast thou made them all: the earth is full of thy riches', and : 'I will sing unto the Lord as long as I live : I will sing praise to my God while I have my being. My meditation of him shall be sweet: I will be glad in the Lord' (Ps. civ). What a remarkable breadth of vision the Bible gives to us! Our Saviour Himself bids us 'consider' the lilies, turn our eyes upon them in order that we might learn more of the Father's care. Let us make sure that our attitude to things is one of positive enjoyment and thankfulness to the One from whom comes 'every good gift and every perfect gift'.

FOOD AND CLOTHING

Taking no thought for what we eat or drink or put on does not mean that Christians are to eat irregular meals, or to become emaciated ascetics, or to dress scruffily and dowdily. It is possible for Christians to go so far in this direction that they behave un-scripturally. I remember a student whose work and health suffered because he regarded it as bad stewardship to eat the meals which the college pro-vided, and instead would take small meals in snack bars in the town. He so economized on fuel that his friends all shivered with cold when they visited him. Self-discipline and self-denial are too little practised among Christians, but we must be careful lest we drift into a false doctrine of asceticism.

It is said of the early Christians that they 'did eat their meat with gladness and singleness of heart' (Acts ii.46). There is nothing wrong with enjoying your food (God has made eating pleasurable), but it is that we are not to be in constant anxiety about it. We are not to live to eat! Table manners are not beneath our attention, for often our behaviour at table reveals the true extent of sanctification. If we know our hearts, then we know it is not only children who go for the largest and tastiest cakes, and gobble them in order to get a second one. I once visited a residence with a very high proportion of divinity students: the way in which they grabbed and gobbled up their food was one of the most appalling performances I have ever witnessed.

Eli and his sons failed in this matter of greed for food: 'Why then look with greedy eye at my sacri-fices . . . by fattening yourselves upon the choicest parts of every offering?' (1 Sa. ii.29, RSV), while Samuel's sons failed because of their greed for gain (viii.3). Greed for food is a common failing in us. The witness of a certain Christian was noticed simply because he did not take the good potato and leave the blackened one for his neighbour. It is by such little acts of self-sacrifice that men show their true allegiance.

It is certainly true that some people live for clothes, and are perpetually anxious about their personal appearance. Peter has some very definite things to say about the adornment of women. Again, this is no reason for scruffiness and dowdiness, or for crimes against good taste or colour sense; for people can honour God even in the way they dress by being pleasing and tidy. It is all a matter of maintaining a proper balance in the amount of money we may justifiably spend on our appearance. It is quite possible for Christians to be extravagant in matters of dress, and in the prices they pay for suits or dresses, ties or shirts. To repentant people asking what practical action they can take, John the Baptist says, 'He that hath two coats, let him impart to him that hath none; and he that hath meat, let him do likewise' (Lk. iii.11). This may well mean, in these days, going to a cheaper tailor and to cheaper restaurants, and giving more to the Lord's work. It is a little staggering sometimes to discover how much some otherwise consistent Christians will regularly pay for meals.

THEFT

There are many 'respectable' ways of stealing—without actually committing theft—which are in vogue today. For some reason people feel at liberty to call theft by other names if they rob a corporation, or company, or if they defraud the Revenue department : in some circles it is even considered clever to evade Customs duty. Certain items are often conveniently omitted from Income Tax returns. But Scripture says: 'For this cause pay ye tribute also ... render therefore to all their dues : tribute to whom tribute is due ; custom to whom custom' (Rom. xiii. 6–8). The road and rail transport companies are constantly cheated by people who avoid payment or who stay on board beyond the stop to which they have paid. Underpaying and overcharging are as much theft as burglary is, even though they may be considered more respectable. It is possible to 'sponge' on the hospitality of those who can ill afford it. Should we sell articles like motor bikes or textbooks for a higher price than we know them to be worth? Do we keep quiet about the hidden snag that we hope they won't notice? Even Christian libraries lose books; how many books that do not belong to us are sitting on our shelves waiting to be returned? If we fail to pay bills promptly, we are enjoying the use of money which really belongs to someone else. Duties must always come before optional pleasures. We must not enjoy any unnecessary extras while outstanding debts are still unpaid.

If we are students on grants from the government, county, university or our parents, are we not robbing them if we fail to work our hardest? As employees we are stealing from our employers if we arrive late or leave early, or if we fail to work our hardest during working hours. There is often a great deal of talk these days about workers' rights, but very little about the rights of those for whom they work. It is far from easy for a man on a gang to work when all the rest knock off, and yet the Bible would seem to imply from its injunctions to slaves that we must work our hardest and our best.

When Zacchaeus received Christ into his home, one of the things which impresses us at once is the new attitude which he has to money. 'Behold, Lord, the half of my goods I give to the poor; and if I have taken any thing from any man by false accusation, I restore him fourfold' (Lk. xix.8). Thus restitution for wrongs done is a mark of our new relationship with Christ, and money, books, stationery, laboratory equipment, etc., may have to be returned to their rightful owners.

THE SNARE OF RICHES

It may be that God does bless us with some small or great portion of wealth. This can be a tremendous blessing, if used to the glory of God. Not every rich young ruler is asked to give all that he has to the poor. But those who are rich in this world are charged not to adopt a superior attitude towards their fellow men, 'nor to trust in uncertain riches, but in the living God, who giveth us richly all things to enjoy'; for men can come to trust the power of their money instead of relying upon God, while God means them to enjoy His gifts. Paul continues with the reminder that those who are so placed are to 'do good, that they be rich in good works, ready to distribute, willing to communicate' (1 Tim. vi. 17, 18). But the wealthy man has a tremendous responsibility and there are greater dangers for him than for his poorer brother: 'Godliness with contentment is great gain. For we brought nothing into this world, and it is

certain we can carry nothing out. And having food
and raiment let us be therewith content. But they
that will be rich fall into temptation and a snare,
and into many foolish and hurtful lusts . . . for the
love of money is the root of all evil' (1 Tim. vi.6–10).

It is not always easy for those who are less well off
to be content with food and raiment. We see others
possessing things which we are unable to enjoy. It is
hard to be satisfied with such things as we have under
such circumstances. Perhaps up till now we have
always been content; but as we begin our careers or
settle down in early married life we dream of lovely
houses and gardens, a good car, contemporary furniture, lovely interior decorating—and contentment
seems far harder. The young men and women of
today are easily infected by the materialism preva-
lent around them—like young Lot, who left the hard
pilgrim path for the comfort and security of Sodom.
Is this why many turn back from the mission field;
because they prefer the comfort of the home country? The cares and riches of this life are the weeds
which choke out the potential fruitfulness of many
a promising shoot. Let us remember the poverty of
the Lord Jesus, who had nowhere to lay His head,
who had to borrow a boat, a donkey, a penny and
even a tomb. Are we content with food and raiment,
or are we out to get a larger car, and a larger house,
as our income increases? There is a challenge here to
live as simply as we may, commensurate with our
professional position; and rejoice in having all the
more to give. There was a case recently of a Christian man in a high position who, when he died, was
still living in the small town into which he had moved

at the time of his marriage, and who had never bought a car. All this, that he might give more to Christian work.

There are no pockets in shrouds. Let us take care lest, in a day when we are concerned only with increasing material gains, God says to us, 'Thou fool, this night thy soul shall be required of thee . . . so is he that layeth up treasure for himself, and is not rich toward God' (Lk. xii. 20, 21).

Covetousness is a constant snare laid for all our feet.

GENEROSITY AND HOSPITALITY

'It is more blessed to give than to receive' and Scripture has much to say about the necessity of giving things to others for their enjoyment. Generosity (translated 'goodness' in the AV) is one of those qualities which is the fruit of the Spirit (Gal. v.22). There are some scathing words in the New Testament for those who are indifferent to the needs of others. 'But if any one has the world's goods and sees his brother in need, yet closes his heart against him, how does God's love abide in him?' (1 Jn. iii.17, RSV). Such concern for the needs of others is expected to be material kindness and not merely pious phrases : 'If a brother or sister be naked, and destitute of daily food, and one of you say unto them, Depart in peace, be ye warmed and filled; notwithstanding ye give them not those things which are needful to the body; what doth it profit ?' (Jas. ii. 15, 16). This, incidentally, raises the issue, to what extent are Christians justified in giving only to mission causes and withholding their money from philanthropy and 'charities' in general? If we have a responsibility to mankind in general, 'Do good unto all men, especially unto them who are of the household of faith', then these good causes should also be matters of some concern to us.

The hospitality of Christian homes can be a very real witness to Christ, although it often entails sacrifice of privacy and leisure. 'Be not forgetful to entertain strangers : for thereby some have entertained angels unawares' (Heb. xiii.2). The Christian is to be one who is 'distributing to the necessity of saints; given to hospitality' (Rom. xii.13). If we really want to get to know people then we can do it best of all in our homes. Extra trouble taken because we have invited someone to stay may be greatly used to the glory of God. Are our homes going to be like that? Are they places where Christians and others may find blessing and rest, like the house Beautiful at which Pilgrim was so refreshed?

The extra thought taken in selecting some gift to please a mother, a wife or a child is all pleasing to the Lord who is Himself the great Giver. The young Christian, through seeing the need to steward his money carefully, may easily become mean and stingy. While we are right to discipline ourselves, we must not forget to be generous to others. While the purchase of a bunch of flowers for oneself might be an indulgence, as a gift to a hostess, to a mother or a wife, it might be the right and courteous thing.

It also takes grace to receive a gift graciously, for sometimes it may be hurtful to our pride to accept, if we are in poor circumstances. We need a heart which responds quickly and graciously to the generosity of others, and we need to be able to express a very real, enthusiastic appreciation of a kindness. The 'Oh I couldn't possibly . . .' convention is usually sheer hypocrisy, and often begins a foolish exchange of 'Really I couldn't . . .' which finally ends with a reluctant acceptance of the gift with diminished grace, which has lessened the other person's joy in giving freely. Let us learn to show a real and proper appreciation of the kindness of others.

CHRISTIAN GIVING

It is God who gives us richly all things to enjoy. It is God who puts us into a family which may be rich or poor. It is God who gives the talents and ability to gain qualifications which make our services of value. It is always God who gives. And this means, therefore, that whatever money we may hold, we hold in trust for God. And so it is possible to steal from God. 'Will a man rob God? Yet ye have robbed me. But ye say, Wherein have we robbed thee? In tithes and offerings' (Mal. iii.8 ff.). Do we only give to God that which costs us nothing to give? (See 2 Sa. xxiv.24.) The money that we have to spare, the odd coins that we have in our pocket or purse? A tithe, even, that we hardly miss, or realize we have given. It is possible to rob God. Ten men who give as little as a tenth, a tithe, can support one Christian worker between them. Yet how much Christian work is crippled for lack of funds : to what dishonouring begging for money, to what appeals and so forth are some Christian Societies forced to resort, and all because Christians themselves are not really doing their utmost in this respect. The most obvious conclusion to be drawn from the lack of funds is that men are robbing God.[1]

There is a wonderful promise which we might all claim for ourselves in this matter : 'God is able to provide you with every blessing in abundance, so that you may always have enough of everything and may provide in abundance for every good work' (2 Cor. ix.8, RSV). This should surely sum up our attitude to things : that God will always provide us enough for our own needs and also enough to provide in abundance for the needs of others.

[1] See the late Fred Mitchell's excellent book, *The Stewardship of Money* (I.V.F.) for a fuller treatment of this whole matter.

CHAPTER VIII

WORDS

'O GENERATION of vipers, how can ye, being evil, speak good things? for out of the abundance of the heart the mouth speaketh. A good man out of the good treasure of the heart bringeth forth good things : and an evil man out of the evil treasure bringeth forth evil things. But I say unto you, That every idle word that men shall speak, they shall give account thereof in the day of judgment. For by thy words thou shalt be justified, and by thy words thou shalt be condemned' (Mt. xii.34–37).

In the previous chapters we have thought of our behaviour in our homes, and with men and with women, and here we see that it is by our words that we please or offend, as much as by our deeds. Our Lord Himself so spoke that they 'wondered at the gracious words which proceeded out of his mouth' (Lk. iv.22). There is a wonderful wholesomeness about every word which fell from His lips, in His dealings with men and women. As Christians we are expected to reveal by our words that this same Lord has put His Spirit within our hearts. Yet how hard we find it to control this little member ! We can only agree with James' conclusion (Jas. iii) that 'if any man offend not in word, the same is a perfect man, and able also to bridle the whole body'. Even the greatest Christians have failed here. Peter is portrayed in the Gospels as one who often blurted out rash words without a thought. Even Paul retracted his words of anger to the high priest (Acts xxiii.5). How can we deal with this deadly poison, this unruly evil? Deal with it we must, as we see from the solemn words of Christ at the beginning of this chapter. But it is well to realize from the start how easily we all fail here and be very merciful towards others who offend in this respect.

The law stated simply: 'Thou shalt not bear false witness', and some consideration of this will bring us to the point of seeing that it is a failure to reverence truth which underlies so many of our idle words.

KEEPING TO THE TRUTH

The Bible does not hesitate to show some of its greatest heroes failing to keep to the truth when the truth is embarrassing. Abraham, Isaac, David and Peter all spring to mind at once. It is equally easy for us to fall into the same snare: but much of our failure in this respect is less obvious than theirs.

There is a danger that prayer letters or missionary talks may give a false impression: we want to give the most glowing report that we can. Sometimes one discovers that a report of conversions has been considerably exaggerated. Alternatively, a picture may be painted too blackly, to give an impression of its difficulties. There is great talk of pagan darkness, or of dreadful heathen customs which are often not much worse than some aspects of life in our own land.

Thinking of the rash avowal of Peter, 'though all men shall be offended because of thee, yet will I never be offended' (Mt. xxvi.33), one is reminded that it is very easy to speak and pray rashly. On occasions one hears wild and unrealistic prayers, which are sometimes said to be 'prayers of faith'; but is it honest to pray for (to take an example) the conversion of everyone who comes to the meeting tonight, when we know that in the will of God not everyone will repent? Often, in youthful enthusiasm no doubt, we pray in terms which are manifestly exaggerated. The same may be true in the words we express to others. Certainly we are men of little faith, but this is not to be remedied by a spate of high-sounding phrases—a sort of spiritual bragging. 'For the kingdom of God does not consist in talk but in power' (1 Cor. iv.20, RSV).

Is it right to invent fictional sermon illustrations and present them as actual fact? Is the gospel really helped by untrue stories? It is worth considering whether some pulpit histrionics do not represent a failure to be true to one's real feelings. Are we always honest about our own Christian experience, or do we describe what we think we ought to feel? Some of the difficulties of young Christians arise from the mode of speech of some Christians, which may give a misleading impression; the expressions 'The Lord told me . . .' or 'The Lord spoke to me . . .' give the impression that we heard a sound, when what we mean is that we have become conscious of His will and grasped His meaning through the voice of Scripture or of conscience.

Are we honest in our exposition of Scripture? Do we sometimes use verses out of context or ones that we know are inaccurate translations because they happen to say what we want to say, and to fit in with our ideas. 'We are not as many, which corrupt the word of God: but as of sincerity . . . speak we in Christ.' 'But have renounced the hidden things of dishonesty, not walking in craftiness, nor handling the word of God deceitfully; but by manifestation of the truth commending ourselves to every man's conscience in the sight of God' (2 Cor. ii.17, iv.2). It is essential that we should be honest and not force upon Scripture interpretations which it will not bear. It is only honest, too, to face up to those difficulties in the Bible or in doctrine which are raised by others, and not quietly to bypass the problems. We have nothing to fear from the truth, and the approach which refuses to face problems honestly will not commend the truth to others.

There is likewise a need to keep to the truth in our work and in our examinations. It is quite easy to be deceitful and to mention something in passing as though we knew all about it, when in fact we know nothing. It is easy for a student to fall into the habits of non-Christians where his work is concerned.

KEEPING PROMISES

The Psalmist speaks of the one who is fit to dwell in the Tabernacle of God as one who 'sweareth unto his neighbour, and disappointeth him not : though it were to his own hindrance' (Ps. xv.5, Prayer Book Version). Yet how commonly Christians break appointments or cancel engagements at the last minute. Frequently students book for conferences and campaigns and then cry off at the last minute, or even just fail to turn up! Speaking engagements are accepted and then at the last minute a telephone call comes to say that it cannot be done. Surely if we have given our word, then the biblical principle given above provides clear 'guidance' that we must

keep our promises however inconvenient it may be
to do so, unless very exceptional circumstances indeed make a change of plans essential. 'Let your
communication be, Yea, yea; Nay, nay' (Mt. v.37).
It is this integrity of the Christian's word once given
which must be maintained, for the Christian's word
is his oath. Christians sometimes make very easy
promises, 'I will send you such and such', 'I will write
to you tomorrow', 'I will pray for you', which they
fail to keep. Next time we promise to give or to send
something to someone, let us remember the proverb
'like clouds and wind without rain is a man who
boasts of a gift he does not give' (Pr. xxv.14, RSV).

KEEPING CONFIDENCES

We are sometimes given information which is really
private, but shared with us by a friend who trusts us,
or who perhaps does not realize that what he is passing on is meant to be confidential. When we have
some such interesting piece of private information, it
is very tempting to want to pass it on, but that is not
Christian. 'He who goes about as a talebearer reveals
secrets, but he who is trustworthy in spirit keeps a
thing hidden' (Pr. xi.13, RSV). This sort of thing so
easily leads to gossip in which a little truth is mingled
with a great deal of speculation, and not a little very
unpleasant suggestion, about the private affairs of
others. Paul speaks of those who are 'not only idle,
but tattlers also and busybodies speaking things
which they ought not' (1 Tim. v.13), and while we
may think that this refers only to widowed ladies or
elderly spinsters, it is true to say that men are often
no less culpable.

Perhaps we are too eager to talk about our differ-

ences with others, and to justify ourselves before a
third party; 'Argue your case with your neighbour
himself, and do not disclose another's secret' (Pr.
xxv.9, RSV). Many Christians are notoriously bad
about the keeping of confidences.

KEEPING CALM

Paul tells us that love is slow to take offence. When
someone is being deliberately provocative it is hard
to keep calm. 'The vexation of a fool is known at
once, but the prudent man ignores an insult' (Pr.
xii.16, RSV). It usually takes two people to make a
quarrel, and 'a soft answer turns away wrath, but a
harsh word stirs up anger' (Pr. xv.1, RSV). There is
an outstanding example of this in Judges viii.1–3,
where Gideon's gracious answer melts the hostility
of the Ephraimites. If others are angry with us, then
we must be 'courteous : not rendering evil for evil, or
railing for railing : but contrariwise blessing' (1 Pet.
iii.9). We need to learn to change the subject
graciously to avoid profitless discussion and heated
argument, 'but foolish and unlearned questions
avoid, knowing that they do gender strifes' (2 Tim.
ii.23). There is, of course, a right and proper place
for contending earnestly for the faith, but it is
horribly possible to do the right thing in the wrong
way. Sometimes we fall into the snare of being con-
tentious—we deliberately put up ideas in order to
start an argument : we begin in a warlike, dogmatic
way, spoiling for a fight, hoping that the other fellow
will rise to the bait. Often we are more concerned
to state our own opinion than to state God's truth.
We just want to put the other fellow in the wrong.
Such contentiousness is constantly reproved in the

New Testament. James speaks of the need for his beloved brethren to be 'swift to hear, slow to speak, slow to wrath' (Jas. i.19), and so many of our failures result from rushing in indignantly without pausing to think.

TALKING TOO SOON

The Psalmist prays 'Set a watch, O Lord, before my mouth; keep the door of my lips' (cxli.3). So many of our biggest bricks result from our failure to pray that God will keep us in this matter. The 'strong, silent man' is a figure of fun, but it takes a strong man to be silent when the matter under discussion is controversial, or when he is not appreciated, and when tempers begin to rise. 'He who utters slander is a fool. When words are many, transgression is not lacking, but he who restrains his lips is prudent' (Pr. x.18, 19, RSV). 'The mind of the righteous ponders how to answer, but the mouth of the wicked pours out evil things' (Pr. xv.28, RSV).

When others do speak foolishly, then we can often cover it up by ignoring it. 'Hatred stirs up strife, but love covers all offences' (Pr. x.12, RSV). Wise words, too, will make a conversation take a profitable turn. 'There is one whose rash words are like sword thrusts, but the tongue of the wise brings healing' (Pr. xii.18, RSV).

Others sometimes make incorrect or inaccurate statements, and we often rush in to correct them and to show that we know better, and that they are wrong. 'A prudent man conceals his knowledge, but fools proclaim their folly' (Pr. xii.23, RSV). So often we could let the matter pass without drawing attention publicly to the other person's mistake and our

own superior knowledge. Some of us can take a delight in contradicting others. It was said of Benjamin
Franklin: 'Once when Franklin was a blundering
youth an old Quaker friend took him aside and
lashed him with a few stinging truths: Ben, your
opinions have a slap in them for everyone who differs
from you . . . you know so much that no man can tell
you anything. Indeed no man is going to try, for the
effort would lead only to discomfort. So you are not
likely ever to know more than you know now, which
is very little.' Franklin then says, 'I made it a rule to
forbear all direct contradiction to the sentiments of
others, and all positive assertion of my own. I even
forbad myself the use of every expression that im-
ported a fix'd opinion, such as "certainly", "un-
doubtedly", etc. and I adopted instead "I conceive"
a thing to be so; or "it so appears to me at present".
When another asserted something I conceived to be
an error, I deny'd myself the pleasure of contradicting him abruptly, and of showing immediately some
absurdity in his proposition, and in answering I
began by observing that in certain cases or circumstances his opinion would be right, but in the present
case there seem'd to me some difference.'[1]

We need to be slow, too, to speak in self-justifica-
tion, but to hear all that is said and to see whether
there is not, after all, some truth in it. 'The way of a
fool is right in his own eyes, but a wise man listens to
advice.'

TALKING TOO MUCH

The fact of the matter is that many of us talk far too
much! One cannot help smiling at Solomon's words,

[1] Dale Carnegie, *How to Win Friends and Influence People.*

'He that hath knowledge spareth his words : . . . even a fool, when he holdeth his peace, is counted wise : and he that shutteth his lips is esteemed a man of understanding' (Pr. xvii. 27, 28). Our frequent attitude is well pilloried by Dale Carnegie, as follows : 'Never listen to anyone for long. Talk incessantly about yourself. If you have an idea while the other fellow is talking, don't wait for him to finish. He isn't as smart as you. Why waste your time listening to his idle chatter? Bust right in and interrupt him in the middle of a sentence.' Did that make you wince, I wonder? I certainly did. 'A fool takes no pleasure in understanding, but only in expressing his opinion' Pr. xviii. 2, RSV). What bad listeners we are— always thinking about what we are going to say next and not really listening to what the other fellow has to say. This kind of discourtesy is bad at any time, but even worse in a conversation with a non-Christian, if we refuse to let him express his opinions. In personal soulwinning we are often ineffective because we are more interested in what we want to say than in what the other person wants to say. Sometimes we may even be irritated because he is contradicting *us*, rather than grieved because he will not turn to God. We must take care lest we merely appear self-assertive, talking about the gospel because we are self-opinionated. Often we can get much further if we ask questions and allow the other person to expose the weakness of his position and to exhaust the feeble store of arguments which is keeping him from Christ.

It is surely a Christian quality to allow others to talk, and, indeed, to seek to draw them out and make them talk. 'The purpose in a man's mind is like deep

water, but a man of understanding will draw it out'
(Pr. xx.5, RSV). Sometimes shy people will sit very
quietly, and we can be a real help if we stop doing
all the talking ourselves, turn from other talkers and
encourage the less assured person to make his own
contribution to the discussion.

'Let another praise you, and not your own mouth'
(Pr. xxvii.2, RSV). Let us take care we do not talk
only about ourselves, our own activities, our own
work, our own interests. It is not a bad idea to take
stock sometimes and to check up on who and what
we have been talking about with someone else—how
much of it was really all about myself?

HUMOUR

There is a great deal of humour in the Bible. Remember the sluggards in Proverbs: one is too lazy
even to lift a hand to his mouth with the next mouth-
ful of food, another turns on his bed like a door on its
hinges, while a third will not go out because of the
remote possibility of there being a lion in the street.
Our Lord's remark about those who strain out gnats
from their drink, but fail to notice the enormous
camel they are in the process of swallowing, must
have brought smiles to the faces of the hearers. But
much of our humour has as its basis half-truths, and
exaggerations of some parts of the truth together with
the suppression of other facts. A great deal of
modern humorous conversation is very shallow and
superficial, and though it may be witty, much of it
is a matter of scoring off some other person who is
not so quick at repartee. Much of our modern radio
humour is scripted so that someone is always the butt
of another's wit. It is easy for malice to creep into this

kind of humour in ordinary life, and it may be very hurtful.

There are times when an amusing remark may break a tense atmosphere, but there are other times when our jokes may spoil a profitable conversation. There is a happy kind of humour which redeems discouragement and disappointment : a tremendous asset in the face of difficulty. There is also a horrible, hearty, uproarious, backslapping type of irresponsible humour which is incapable of discussing anything seriously. How often serious thoughts are distracted by some one of us foolishly introducing some funny element into the discussion. 'A merry heart doeth good like a medicine' (Pr. xvii.22), but we can have an overdose !

GREETINGS AND COMPLIMENTS

So many of our conventional greetings can be given in such a way as to negate their effect : 'Thank you' can really mean something, or it can be a mere matter of form. Courtesy and politeness are not the same thing. People can be icily or smoothly polite, while giving the impression that they are bored and thoroughly disgusted. I once knew a man who used to reply politely 'How grand' to any remark, but in such a way as to imply the reverse.

Greetings like 'Good morning' can often pave the way for a deeper friendship. They are especially important to those who serve us, to shopkeepers and to others whom we meet as a matter of routine; and especially to overseas students, who consider it the height of rudeness if we do not greet them. There is, of course, a real place for a kind and appreciative word to others. 'A word fitly spoken is like apples of gold in a setting of silver' (Pr. xxv.11, RSV). We should learn to be appreciative of others. We need the opposite attitude to that of 'Lifemanship', which aims to make the other fellow feel uncomfortable and to score off him (a thoroughly unpleasant game!)—but as Christians we should rather endeavour to make others feel at home. There is a lovely story about H. C. Trumbull, who believed that we should always find something about another person to commend and to compliment him upon. On one occasion he was offered a drink from a large flask of whisky by a fellow passenger on the train. He declined, but thanked the man warmly for his generosity.

'Don't you ever drink, my friend?'

'No, my friend, I do not.'

'Well, I guess you think I'm a pretty rough fellow.'

'I think you are a very generous hearted fellow. But I tell you frankly, I don't think your whisky drinking is the best thing about you.'

'Well, I don't believe it is.'

It was this positive attitude of Trumbull's which made him so much loved and so much used to win others for Christ.

We must of course be careful that we do not go to the other extreme of flattery and be guilty of insincerity. Isaiah looks forward to the end of flattery, when 'The fool will no more be called noble, nor the knave said to be honourable' (xxxii.5, RSV). Christians are sometimes guilty of this kind of insincerity when introducing a speaker at a meeting. It is pointless to build him up too much, because if he is poor

then it is an anticlimax, and if he is good it is unnecessary. Such treatment may be very embarrassing for a modest man, and very bad for a proud one.
'A man that flattereth his neighbour spreadeth a net
for his feet' (Pr. xxix.5). A few honest words of real
appreciation are sweet, but flattery is useless. 'It is
not good to eat much honey, so be sparing of com-
plimentary words' (Pr. xxv.27, RSV).

HEALTHFUL SPEECH

The Bible does far more than simply tell us to avoid
untruthfulness and insincerity. It suggests that our
speech should be winsome, wholesome and healthful
in a positive way. 'The mouth of the righteous is a
fountain of life' (Pr. x.11, RSV). One thinks of people
with whom it is always a joy to converse : not because they necessarily always speak on religious
themes, for they do not : but because their conversation is interesting and positive. 'Let your speech be
alway with grace, seasoned with salt' (Col. iv.6).
'Let no corrupt communication proceed out of your
mouth, but that which is good to the use of edifying,
that it may minister grace unto the hearers' (Eph.
iv.29). This last verse is in an interesting context—
that of grieving the Spirit. The reason would seem
to be that it is especially grieving to the Holy Spirit,
who is the inspirer of Christian utterance, that we
should defile our mouths with corrupt speech.
'Pleasant words', says Solomon, 'are like a honey-
comb, sweetness to the soul and health to the body'
(Pr. xvi.24, RSV). We need to pray that all our utterance may be pleasant and pleasing. 'To make an apt
answer is a joy to a man, and a word in season, how

good it is!' (Pr. xv.23, RSV). A good Christian conversationalist is something which we should make it our prayers to become, that, as they wondered at our Master, they might take note of the gracious words which proceed out of our mouths.

CHAPTER IX

THOUGHTS

THE last of the Ten Commandments makes it clear that God is not content with half measures. His moral demands extend to the mind and to the innermost thoughts of the heart. He is a God who desires truth in the inward parts. The Lord Jesus says that it is the things that come from within, out of the heart of man, which defile a man (Mt. xv.10–20). It is common to hear of young Christians troubled by temptations, who have been comforted by the statement, a true one, that you cannot stop birds flying over your head, but you can stop them building nests in your hair! To be tempted is not to have sinned; sin comes when temptation is welcomed into the mind. But very often it is. This is the problem of which the young Christian is so immediately aware: that though he now has a new allegiance to Christ, his very mind and heart is corrupt and sinful. We must be careful that we do not give to such new disciples the impression that provided they do not allow sinful words and actions they are beating temptation. It is possible to sin with our minds. Proverbs xxiv.9, 'The thought of foolishness is sin . . .', reads in the RSV as 'The devising of folly is sin'. To cherish in our hearts deliberately hateful or lustful thoughts, to turn them over in our minds instead of turning them out: this is sin.

Indeed the real battleground *is* within, in our minds, for our words and deeds are merely the outward expressions of the inward mind, out of which proceed all the things which defile a man. All the matters that we have discussed in the previous chapters will only come right if we pay attention not only to them but to our minds and thoughts as well. It is not enough that our bodies and tongues be apparently controlled, and our words and deeds apparently consistent with our Christian profession. The battle must be carried into the very citadel of our hearts and minds. If there is a focus of infection within, then our treatment of the outward symptoms will afford only partial and temporary relief.

We must not overlook the importance of the mind in seeking to practise consistent Christianity. It is possible for a man or woman to be very correct in outward things, to have all the jargon and all the behaviourisms of Christians—and yet to permit in himself or herself a lazy, undisciplined, impure and even chaotic mind. The public life may apparently be a model of consistency, and yet the private thoughts a riot of impurity and malice. Is it not here that we need the saving work of Christ most of all— that we may be 'transformed by the renewing of our minds' (see Rom. xii.2)? 'Be renewed in the spirit of your mind' (Eph. iv.23), says Paul. 'Create in me a clean heart', prays David (Ps. li. 10). When Naaman's leprosy was cleansed, his flesh became like that of a little child (2 Ki. v. 14). Oh, for minds and hearts made perfectly clean like that!

I take this commandment, then, as a reminder that it is not enough to watch our deeds and words only. If we are to be fruitful in *every* good work, then we must seek to bring the whole realm of mind and thoughts under the rule of Christ.

PRIDE

Pride is repeatedly mentioned in Scripture as one of the things which comes out of the heart and defiles a man. 'Every one that is proud in heart is an abomination to the Lord' (Pr. xvi.5). It is here that we begin to see something of the terrible sinfulness of sin and of its grip upon us. Even the best things in life may be blighted by this. At our highest moments of achievement for God, loathsome thoughts of self-congratulation come flooding in. How often have our efforts to serve God been marred because our motives were at fault. We were more concerned with the effect which our action would produce, than with the glory it would bring to God. We were more concerned with what people would think of *us*, than with what they would think about God. We wanted people to think of our ingenious approach, our clever illustrations, our polished utterance, instead of being concerned that they should meet Christ, and that their loyalty to Him should be deepened.

Many of the faults we have already discussed find their roots here : pride of race and colour, pride of family and culture, pride of intellect, pride of physique, pride of face, pride of denomination and, worst of all, pride of grace, spiritual pride, pride in our devotion, in our service, in our spiritual gifts. What a hateful, blighting thing it is. It is a danger for the young Christian. Paul speaks of the danger for such a person in being given responsibility too early. 'Not a novice, lest being lifted up with pride he fall into the condemnation of the devil' (1 Tim. iii.6). Over and over again the Epistles warn of the

danger of being 'blown up with conceit'. How easy
it is for the Christian student, on a committee maybe,
to be in this way 'puffed up'. We can be puffed up
because we think we are more enlightened than
others (1 Cor. viii.1), or because we belong to some
group or other having some special emphasis (Col.
ii.18).

How often pride leads to other sins : to anger because our pride is hurt, for instance. We thought
that we should have been included in that committee, they might at least have consulted us. Pride leads
to self pity. Pride leads us to a foolish refusal to give
in, and we go on hurting and being hurt because of
our pride. It was pride that made poor Jonah angry
when he sulked beneath his gourd. He had been
made to look a fool; his prophecy was not going to
be fulfilled because God had had mercy on the
repentant people of Nineveh. That is typical of
pride; we had rather that others were out of the
mercy of God than that we should be humiliated.
'Doest thou well to be angry?' comes the quiet
reasoning voice of the Lord.

When we consider our Lord's humility, being
made in the likeness of men, taking the form of a
servant (Phil. ii.5-11), and His girding of Himself
with a towel to wash the disciples' feet (Jn. xiii), then
we should see our own great sinfulness. 'Whoever
would be great among you must be your servant, and
whoever would be first among you must be slave of
all' (Mk. x. 43, 44, RSV). It is pride that keeps us
from getting up to perform many a menial duty : let
my mother do it; let my wife do it; only let somebody else do it, it is beneath my dignity. So often
we expect others to minister to us, to our needs, to

our pride and to pander to our desires, but 'the Son of man came not to be ministered unto, but to minister, and to give his life . . .', and 'the servant is not greater than his Lord'. But how hard we find it to take the lowly and despised place! Pride may allow us to do it, if our 'humility' is sure to be noticed; but if not, our pride demands that others should realize how humble we are!

Humility is the mainspring of all courtesy. The proud can be polite, but not courteous. It is interesting that the one word translated 'courteous' in the New Testament (from the Received Text) is in fact best translated 'humbleminded' (1 Pet. iii.8). Pride is thus the enemy of true courtesy. Love, we read, is not puffed up (1 Cor. xiii.4), but how hard we find it to avoid this danger. There is an encouragement for us in 1 Peter v, where we are told 'God resisteth the proud, and giveth grace to the humble', i.e. God always seeks to abase those who exalt themselves, but to those who do abase themselves He gives grace, that they may thus become more truly humble.

ENVY

Envy is another of the things which is listed among the works of the flesh. Again it is coveting, but it is usually concerned with reputation or advantage. It is especially hateful when a Christian is tempted to envy the usefulness of another Christian. The attitude of the Prodigal's elder brother is typical of the envious attitude; 'and he was angry, and would not go in'. The older Christian may be envious of some younger Christian, who seems to be preferred before him. Immediately we say 'Why wasn't I chosen? Everybody takes more notice of him than they do of me'; just as a child may envy the new baby who seems to be getting all the attention. We envy another's talents, intellectual ability, his games ability, his success with the opposite sex, his spiritual progress, his promotion, his popularity. We may be envious of one who shows us up, as Cain was envious of Abel . . . 'we should love one another. Not as Cain, who was of that wicked one, and slew his brother. And wherefore slew he him? Because his own works were evil, and his brother's righteous' (1 Jn. iii.11, 12). The patriarchs, moved with envy, sold Joseph. It was for envy that the Pharisees delivered up the Lord Jesus.

Once envy has taken hold of us, it blinds our judgment and spoils our relationships. Nothing the other person can do is right; we hate his voice, we despise his expressions and, underneath it all, we seethe with envy. We run down those whom we envy before others, or damn them with faint praise. Everything they do seems to us to be directed against us. We are quick to take offence. Sometimes we want to scream with annoyance. We would rather see men not converted than brought to Christ through the one whom we envy. What a hateful sin this is, and how it blights and cramps our lives. The devil uses it as a favourite means of sowing discord among brethren. Every time a committee is appointed, he gets to work on those who think they might have been on it. Every time a colleague is appointed to a higher position, every time a friend is engaged, the devil starts provoking people to envy. Think of all the personality problems that arise among Christians in churches, in missions, in Christian Unions. What is the root trouble? Envy.

What can we do about it? We must pray for the love of God to be shed abroad in our hearts. We must deliberately crucify envy by praising the other person from the heart, by looking for things to praise and admire. It may prove the right thing to go and confess our fault to the brother concerned (though let us make sure we are not using it as a lever to make him do what we want), for the temptation is sometimes a mutual one, and when we discover this, the adversary's plot is foiled. I remember two of us together on our knees, roaring with laughter, because we had discovered that the enemy had been provoking each of us in exactly the same way to envy the other. The discovery did not completely cure us; but we were aware of the problem, and were then able to pray alone and together for each other, and we are now very fast friends.

SLOTH

This takes many forms; there are the more obvious ways in which we just waste our time; we read a little bit of this, a little bit of that, and never really settle to anything. We may spend time reading stories or novels, instead of getting down to the many other more profitable things we had been planning to do. But there are far more subtle kinds of slothfulness.

There is a lazy mind, which is always making resolutions but always failing to carry them out. Like the Pool of Siloam, we may be superficially moved but without any lasting effect. There is a momentary sense of failure, and we are stirred at some meeting or service; but it is all very superficial, and, like the man who gets a glimpse of himself in the mirror and straightway forgets the sort of person that he was, so we go on our way unchanged. We have failed to 'lay it to heart' (Mal. ii.2). This is the common form of spiritual laziness—we know things but we don't really put them into practice : we know we ought to be reading our Bibles more, ought to be stewarding our money, ought to be regular in intercessory prayer for others, ought to be helping more at home, ought to be . . . whatever it is. But we have a lazy mind, and we dream and doze the hours and days away.

What of our increasing in doctrinal understanding? 'In understanding be men', says Paul, and we keep on meaning to get down to something really solid and worth while, but somehow we have failed to do so. Are we not sometimes intellectually lazy in that we accept uncritically things that we read, or that we hear, without proving them for ourselves? It is those whose senses are exercised by reason of use (Heb. v.14), to discern both good and evil, who are mature. Too easily we accept the ideas current in our own particular group without pausing to ask ourselves whether they are truly scriptural.

The real test of an ordered mind is how disciplined we are in the use of time when we are alone. It is faithfulness in secret over little things which breeds in us the character to be faithful in the big things. It was David's quiet shepherding of the flock and steady practice in defending the flock all alone on the quiet hillsides, which prepared him for the shepherding of Israel amid the tumult of the battle and for the defeat of Goliath.

ANXIETY

This is often a temperamental failing, but it does seem especially common among young people at a certain stage in their lives. Going to school is a matter of course, and going out from the shelter of the home, going up to college or to some further kind of training is often almost as inevitable. National Service has also been something all 'laid on'. But at this point the young man or woman is often having to make the biggest decisions in life. For the first time it is essential to make a really big choice—and we are only too conscious of how important a choice it is. And so, in these years, there is often a sense of insecurity and instability.

Others may feel themselves to be in some particular way mentally or emotionally handicapped; they are afraid of their own instability, afraid that they may not be able to stand the pace, and so they hang back anxiously seeking for some absolutely secure and safe path. Some dither about going to the overseas mission field for years, until it is finally too late. But it is really a time to get a grip on oneself, to 'gird up the loins', and to go out in the power of Christ, seeing life as a great adventure with Him.

The only remedy for all this is to recognize all that one is, in oneself, and not try to be somebody else; and, recognizing one's own weakness, to cast 'all your care upon him; for he careth for you' (1 Pet. v.7). We have to learn to be 'anxious for nothing' and to make our requests known unto Him. We often talk a great deal about the insecurity of the present age, but as we read through the Bible and find out how cheap life was in those days, and how the international situation was in a constant state of flux, then we realize that the Scriptures were written for our comfort, and that the God of all the heroes of Hebrews xi is our God still.

A RENEWED MIND

'Whatsoever things are true . . . honest . . . just . . . pure . . . lovely . . . of good report; if there be any virtue, and if there be any praise, think on these things' (Phil. iv.8). This verse points to the solution of our problem. If the mind is filled with the good and the beautiful, then there will be no room for the evil. But if we fill our minds with the sordid, and the sultry, the cheap and the sugary, then we are heading for trouble. This has a great deal of bearing upon the things we read and converse about, the pictures we see (moving or otherwise), and the things we hear. The press, the radio, television and the cinema seem to delight in portraying the sordid and sinful and the abnormal. All too often they do no good. They merely leave an unpleasant taste in the mouth, and a worse smirch upon the mind. There is a tremendous value in the normal and the healthy and the beautiful. 'Set your affection on things above', seeking the things which are above, would suggest that if we are really to get things into perspective, then we must lift our eyes to God and get our minds attuned to His will.

There is an interesting passage in C. S. Lewis' *That Hideous Strength* in which the demonic forces, working for man's undoing, try to corrupt one of their victims with distorted art. Everything was bent and twisted. But 'as a desert first teaches men to love water, or as absence first reveals affection, there arose up against this background of the sour and crooked, some kind of vision of the sweet and the straight. Something else—something he vaguely called the Normal apparently existed. . . . It was all mixed up with Jane and fried eggs, and soap and sunlight and rooks cawing at Cure Hardy.'[1]

But most of all it is when we realize that only God can deal with a corrupted, sin-besmirched, evil, selfish mind, and give us a new and cleansed mind, that we can begin to put things right. If it is the citadel of the mind which is to be captured by Christ, then we may rejoice that the verse, so often quoted, is in the context of the thoughts and imaginations of the mind. We may be 'mighty through God to the pulling down of strongholds; casting down imaginations, and every high thing that exalteth itself against the knowledge of God, and bringing into captivity every thought to the obedience of Christ' (2 Cor. x. 4, 5). Every thought made new? Can these things be? This conquest in the power of Christ is the subject of the final chapter.

[1] Pan edition, p. 184.

CHAPTER X
'PERFECT IN EVERY GOOD WORK'

IN the preceding chapters we have sought to re-
interpret the commands in the Decalogue, relating
to our duty to our neighbour, in the light of the
New Testament ideal of fruitfulness in every good
work. In his *Essay on the Christian Ministry*, Bishop
Lightfoot makes a rather thrilling statement about
the Christian ideal in terms of time, space and
people. It is 'a holy season extending the whole year
round—a temple confined only by the limits of the
habitable world—a priesthood coextensive with the
human race'. Under the old covenant, the Jews
were instructed to set aside holy days and seasons,
holy places for worship and holy men to offer
sacrifices. But they recognized this to be representative and temporary. The priests and Levites repre-
sented the people as a whole; the heaven of heavens
could not contain the God who consented to mani-
fest Himself to them within the confines of the
earthly sanctuary. But under the new covenant all
is now changed. There is but one great representative
High Priest, and every Christian is a priest who
offers sacrifices of praise and thanksgiving. The sab-
baths, new moons and annual festivals, are likewise
done away with (Col. ii. 16, 17), because they were
only representative of the fact that *all* our time now
belongs to God. The idea of consecrated places is
likewise foreign to the New Testament. In later times

such ideas seem to have crept back into the Church, and we must make up our minds how scriptural they are; but they are a poor substitute for the tremendous conception that seems to have replaced the old order of things. Every moment of time is to be hallowed to an eternal God, every square foot of earth to an omnipresent God and every willing man and woman to the worship and service of a holy God. As Christians, it is our responsibility to glorify Him at all times and in all places and to seek, ourselves, to be holy, even as He is holy.

As Christians, the whole of our life is to be like a watered garden : every section of it is to blossom and bear fruit to the praise of Christ. But as, in the previous chapters, we have reviewed the different relationships and activities that make up our lives, we have been very conscious of much fallow ground that needs to be broken up, much in the way of weed-choked beds, all needing attention if our lives are to be like the garden of the Lord.

GOD'S FINAL PURPOSE

'After those days, saith the Lord, I will put my law in their inward parts, and write it in their hearts' (Je. xxxi.31–34). How we all long for the fulfilment of this great new covenant promise in our own lives, for we cannot but be conscious, over and over again, of the difference between what we know we ought to be, and what we are at this present. The author, working through the various Scriptures himself, feels conscious afresh of his own weakness and failure, and of his own unworthiness to be writing such a book. As the Psalmist, pondering on the law and precepts of God cried, 'O that my ways were directed to keep thy statutes . . . O let me not wander from thy commandments' (Ps. cxix. 5, 10), so do we cry.

God is not satisfied with just patched-up old sinners. He who has begun the good work of grace in us will be satisfied with nothing less than the finishing of it. We know that God, sending 'his own Son . . . for sin', and His Spirit to set us free from the principle of sin and death, has this end in view, 'that the righteousness of the law might be fulfilled in us' (Rom. viii.4). We are not only to be justified by Christ's obedience to the law and fulfilling of it, but so to be sanctified by the work of the indwelling Spirit that the very righteousness of life required by the law is fulfilled in our lives. And so God's great, final purpose is that we should be renewed after the image of Him who created us (Col. iii.10), or 'conformed to the image of his Son, that he might be the firstborn among many brethren' (Rom. viii.29). This is the tremendous goal towards which we should all be striving. For, as John says, those of us who have this hope of being like Him have the urge within us to purify ourselves (1 Jn. iii. 2, 3). But although this book has been largely concerned with the purifying process, we must remember that we are not left to struggle vainly after holiness on our own.

THE INDWELLING SPIRIT

If we tremble and mourn, as we should, that 'this infection of nature doth remain, yea in them that are regenerated' (Article IX of the Thirty-Nine Articles) and that we find ourselves so lacking in the 'righteousness of the law', then we may also rejoice to know that the Holy Spirit is within us to help us in all our infirmities. He is working to produce in us the fruit of the Spirit, the fruits of righteousness and Christian character, which is the reproduction of Christ's own character in us. The Spirit changes us from one degree of glory to another degree of glory, into His likeness (2 Cor. iii.18).

This realization of the indwelling Spirit must not be a purely theoretical doctrinal statement, as it so often is, but a living experience. Thus the late Fred Mitchell, the chemist's assistant who became Home Director of the China Inland Mission, wrote of the impact this made upon his own life : 'Feeling acutely the difference between the life in the church on Sunday and the life in the world on Monday, the truth suddenly laid hold of heart and mind, and life has never been the same since. I saw that "Christ was in me" ; that He was not only my Saviour dying for me on the cross, and my Lord risen from the tomb, but He was my Life dwelling in my heart, and that this was true just then in a smoky railway station, and everywhere else. It dawned upon me that Christ was in me then as I walked down the platform and afterwards down the street ; it was true as I arrived at my place of business and began the work of the day. In short, wherever I was, He was there, in me as my Life. Whatever my need was, He was living within to meet it; whatever my temptation, He was there to defeat it. That was how I discovered how "He saved His people", and me as one of them, "from their sins".' [1] Notice here how Mr Mitchell emphasizes the work of the Spirit in us, in the ordinary humdrum life of every day, in helping us to live it to God's glory.

[1] Phyllis Thompson, *Climbing on Track*, p. 59.

THE PLACE OF WILL

But it is not enough that when faced with our own inconsistency, we should comfort ourselves with the thought that He will make us perfect in every good work to do His will, and that He will be working in us that which is well pleasing in His sight. We cannot leave the matter there. The responsibility cannot just be removed from our shoulders like that. It is those who hunger and thirst after righteousness who will be filled. The working of the Holy Spirit does not remove from us the necessity of desiring and purposing to be conformed to His will. Thus the 'righteousness of the law' is fulfilled in us, 'who walk . . . after the Spirit' (Rom. viii.4). Again, we must walk in the Spirit if we are not to fulfil the lust of the flesh (Gal. v.16). What does it mean to 'walk in the Spirit'? Scripture seems to suggest that this is something which we may, or may not, do. It seems to mean a willing determination to rest in His strength and not in our own, if the victory is to be won. Our own will is not overruled, you see : rather it is undergirded. The Holy Spirit encourages my will, He strengthens it, but He does *not* overrule it, or take it from me. I must, of my own voluntary choice, 'walk in the Spirit'. There must be a real heart-longing on our part for a new and holy character, and we must deliberately choose to act in obedience to His law. God loves obedience. He does not remove from us the joy of obeying Him. We must strive, must put off and put on as His word commands. He lays these responsibilities upon us. But we could not do them by ourselves, apart from Him. The Holy Spirit is the great inspirer of action in the believer. As I act, apparently in accord with the free working of my own will, the Spirit works in me to will and to do of His good pleasure. He works through the faith and action of the believer.

THE PLACE OF DEVOTION

This brings us to a necessary corrective. This book will be of no avail if we all begin to rush hither and thither seeking to be fruitful in every good work in our own strength. Martha was very busy and active in her way. She wanted to be fruitful in her domestic good work. But her service was defective, because it was not balanced properly with a life of devotion. We need to sit at His feet first, and listen to His word, like Mary, if our works are to be really pleasing to Him. Martha was busy trying to *act*, before she first paused to discover exactly what it was that He wanted her to be doing. Our lives must consist of these two complementary elements, of devotion to Him on the one hand, and work for Him on the other. Like the two oars with which a boat is rowed, there must be a balance between them. Too much of one and too little of the other will only cause us to move in circles. If all the accent is on devotion, without our love for Him being shown forth in the practical keeping of His commandments, then we shall make no progress. If all the accent is on activity and works, without the time spent in personal devotion to Him, the result will be the same : sterility. Such a distinction between work and devotion is, of course, only one of convenience. They blend into each other. Work is all the sweeter because it is compounded with the fragrance of devotion. It was said of the twelve that they were chosen 'that they should be

with him, and that he might send them forth . . .'
So it is with ourselves : devotion and service are both
part of His plan for us. It is not that we go into the
secret place with Him, and then go out from Him
into the world. He is with us always. We go out with
Him. As His sheep we go in and out and find pasture
(Jn. x). The Shepherd, to whom we go in, is also the
Shepherd who leads us out.

This devotion is essential, for the kind of Christian
righteousness of which we have been speaking is
something that has to be sought on our knees. If we
are never on our knees, then we shall never find this
righteousness. 'Seek ye first the kingdom of God and
his righteousness', says the Lord Jesus. This is the
divine way of sanctifying us : 'Seek . . .' It is those
who seek, who find. He is a rewarder of them that
diligently seek Him (Heb. xi.6). It is time to seek the
Lord till He come and rain righteousness upon us
(Ho. x.12). The great secret of a harvest of the fruits
of righteousness is to pray for the divine rain. Seeking His presence, and the blessing that must accom-
pany His loving presence, is the secret of Christian
growth. Prayer is thus a means of grace, because in it
we should spend time with Him. When we do, we
begin to acquire His values, and to want for ourselves
what He wants to give us. We begin to share His
hatred of sin and love of holiness. When we do that,
we begin to share His holy character. The secret of
seeking holiness and righteousness, then, is to seek
Him. 'Seek the Lord, and his strength : seek his face
evermore' (Ps. cv.4). If I want to be a consistent
Christian, I must seek Him whose presence makes
inconsistency hateful. If I want to be a fruitful

Christian in every good work, I must seek Him whose Spirit makes fruitfulness possible.

It is Christ, and only Christ, who will enable us to live this new life, for it is He who makes us perfect in every good work to do His will, working in us that which is well pleasing in His sight.

> 'We go' in faith, our own great weakness feeling,
>   And needing more each day Thy grace to know :
>   Yet from our hearts a song of triumph pealing;
>   'We rest on *Thee*, and in Thy name we go.'